HOW TO BUILD A
SMARTER
FASTER
BETTER
ESTATE AGENCY BUSINESS

HOW TO BUILD A
SMARTER FASTER BETTER
ESTATE AGENCY BUSINESS

REGINA MANGAN

ISBN: 9798871612859

Imprint: Independently published

Copyright 2023, Regina Mangan

All views expressed in this book are those of the author and are not intended for use as a definitive guide. This work is owned in full by the primary author, Regina Mangan. No part of this publication may be reproduced or transmitted in any form whatsoever without the written permission of Regina Mangan:

reginaomangan@icloud.com

This book was produced in collaboration with Write Business Results Limited. For more information on their business book and marketing services, please visit www.writebusinessresults.com or contact the team via info@writebusinessresults.com.

ACKNOWLEDGEMENTS

There are so many people I would like to thank. Firstly, my wonderful husband Irial who inspires me every day with his brilliant business acumen.

I am especially grateful for his love and support and how he encourages me to be the best version of myself. He celebrates my accomplishments and gives me the freedom to do what I need to do. Secondly, my son Pierce who gives me purpose, pride and privilege to be his mother. I also want to thank my mother Adelaide for her positive outlook, lessons in life and amazing work ethic and humour.

Acknowledgements

I'd like to thank my first mentor Billy Power who guided me when I was starting out. Over the years Billy has been there for me, and I learnt from Billy how incredibly important it is to have wise sages in your corner. Billy's financial expertise and practical advice have stood me well.

Thank you to Maria, my amazing colleague and friend of 20 years. We have accomplished so much together and we have more to do!

When you have been in business for over 26 years, like I have, there are many people who have had an impact on your life, unfortunately I can't thank you all. Thank you Nora Widger for giving me my first business overdraft and supporting me when I really needed it in the early days.

I'd like to thank Ivan from Write Business Results, who has worked very closely with me to write this book. Your straight-talking, no-nonsense approach was brilliant and greatly appreciated. Thank you to all the Write Business Results team, I couldn't have done this without you.

I would like to say a special thank you and tribute to my amazing mentor and friend, Sanjay Gandhi. You sure have pushed

Acknowledgements

me in the right direction. You encouraged me, no you pushed me, into writing this book. Sanjay Gandhi you are one in a million. One thing is for sure, Sanjay is one of the smartest, straightest talking, most generous people I have the privilege of knowing. I'll be sharing some of Sanjay's teachings throughout this book.

Acknowledgements

I'd like to dedicate my book to my mother Adelaide.

For all the things you say you didn't achieve in life, I'd like you to know you did through me. Thank you mother, I love you dearly. Since you moved to Dungarvan during the pandemic to live near us, I realise I'm more like you than I ever realised.

"Enthusiasm is the baking powder of life. Without it you are flat; with it you rise."

Mammy's favourite quote, which I heard over and over the years.

VI

CONTENTS

Acknowledgements	i
Dedication	v
Foreword	1
Introduction	3
Chapter 1: Smarter, Faster, Better	15
Chapter 2: Values and Mission	37
Chapter 3: Have the Right People on the Bus	60
Chapter 4: Do the Right Thing	91
Chapter 5: Be a Challenger	111
Chapter 6: Develop Your Tribe	139
Chapter 7: Systems and Processes	181

Chapter 8: Mind the Money	207
Chapter 9: Train Hard	229
Chapter 10: Dealing with Bullies and Haters	255
Chapter 11: Live in the Now	277
Chapter 12: Managing Change	295
Conclusion	317
About the Author	322

FOREWORD

BY SANJAY GANDHI

This book is written by Regina Mangan who I have had the pleasure of mentoring one-to-one. What really impresses me about Regina is her can-do attitude and will to succeed.

Regina has run her own estate agency business for over 26 years and her appetite to learn consistently is infectious. She has been a leading realtor in Ireland and the go-to person in Waterford.

Regina has grown her business in Waterford to a point where she has some of the leading technology and best practices admired by her peers.

Foreword

This book can be best described as a recipe for success and I hope it will inspire you to follow in the footsteps of Regina if achieving success is your mantra.

Regina now spends most of her time developing her teams to continue the business growth and is now involved in long-term growth strategy.

Enjoy this book and be sure to connect with Regina.

Reading this book could be your best business decision yet!

Sanjay Gandhi
Mentor / Entrepreneur

INTRODUCTION

I've always wanted to write a book about business. Business is my passion and when it comes to the estate agency business, it's something I know very well. But for many years I didn't tell anyone about this desire to write a book. One person I did open up to, however, was my mentor Sanjay Gandhi – little did I know that telling him about this goal would set me on my way to achieving it.

In 2022, I travelled to a marketing conference with Sanjay and a few of the other agents who are part of the mastermind group he runs. Not only was there a company exhibiting that specialises in helping entrepreneurs write their books, but

Introduction

Sanjay knew Georgia, the founder. He introduced us, I met her and Ivan, another member of her team, and after a few discussions I had committed to writing the book I'd always wanted to share with the world. But that was the easy part.

Once I made the commitment, I started to panic a little. Self-doubt began to creep in. Thoughts like, "Who am I to write a book? Who will read this book? Have I really anything worth saying?" crowded into my mind. I worried that people would laugh at me, or ask the same questions I'd been asking myself – I imagined people saying, "Who does she think she is?" The list of negative self-talk went on and on. I realised I needed some help to pull me out of this downward spiral, which if I'd continued may well have meant you wouldn't be holding this book in your hands.

I decided to speak to two people whose opinions I value – Niamh, an estate agent friend, and Lynda from the Waterford Chamber of Commerce who is a friend, business associate and the most straight-talking person I know. The messaging I received from both of them was overwhelmingly positive. And so here I am writing my book, and here you are reading it. Why have I shared my self-doubt with you right at the beginning of our journey together?

Introduction

Because I think we all fear being judged throughout this process of putting ourselves out there, and I've certainly had a bit of that in my time – but not enough to stop me. I really love Lisa Novak, an Australian estate agency guru. She says, "Change the channel honey" to her critics on social media, and she is so right. So, if you are reading this and you find some of the things in this book helpful then that makes me super happy. If you're reading it and you're one of the haters, then all I can say is thank you for buying my book!

One of the first things I'd like to share with you is that achieving things in life is about first deciding what you want, then setting out a plan and committing to it. As the old saying goes, how do you eat an elephant? Bite by bite.

If you are reading this book, you're likely already running an estate agency business or are considering setting one up. Like me, you enjoy working in residentail property and get a buzz from helping people move forward in their journey. I'm sure that while you love what you do, you are also tired of working incredibly long hours and at times dealing with unreasonable clients.

Introduction

In my 26 years of running a property business, Liberty Blue, I have been there and done that! I've worked crazy hours, answered my phone to clients as I'm going to bed, even struggled to make ends meet at times despite putting in a lot of hard work. I truly do understand the challenges you're facing because I have been there too at some point in my years as an estate agency owner.

But for all the challenges, building my business has been incredibly rewarding and I wouldn't change it for the world. I'm proud to have established Waterford's first property letting and management company, Bookaroom, which later became Liberty Blue Estate Agents. We have achieved exponential growth in the 26 years we've been in business, as well as survived Ireland's worst recession and seen a significant 111% per cent increase in property sales income post Covid-19 pandemic (*compared to 2019). We're proud that, as a business, we are an integral part of the local economy. Our annual contribution of over €1 million to the community exemplifies our belief in the local multiplier effect.

I am always looking for ways to innovate, and improve, to help us move forwards as a business and as individuals. I'm sure

Introduction

you're excited about the next stages of your journey too, which is why you're here.

Let me be clear from the beginning, this is not a book that will take you, step by step, through how to build an estate agency business. There are plenty of other resources that will give you the practical steps you need to take if that's what you're look-ing for. This book will, however, set out the principles that have helped me and my team achieve success with Liberty Blue. It's an honest account of my time working in this industry – I'm not going to pretend I know everything (I certainly don't) or that I've always got everything right (I haven't). Even if, to the outside world, it looks like I have got everything together, I can tell you now that there are times when things are not so smooth behind the scenes.

Appearances can be deceptive

Several years ago, I was a guest speaker at an event run by the Waterford Local Enterprise Board for women in business. I'd had my hair blow dried the day before and I walked in wearing my best dress. On the face of it, I looked like I had everything together – behind the scenes that could not have been further from the truth!

What you couldn't see from my external appearance was that, before I'd left the house, my young son had been sick and I'd had to calm him down, and try to clean up before running out of the door. Just as I thought I had sorted things out I ran back upstairs to grab my phone, bowl of granola and yoghurt in hand, tripped up and spilled the contents of that bowl all over my underwear drawer – how glamorous! The worst part is I knew I'd need to clean that up once I got home as I hadn't had time before I left the house. I told these women this story, and they all laughed and nodded in agreement. You can't see what's going on behind the scenes in someone's life and, more often than not, there's a mess somewhere out of sight that's waiting to be cleared up.

Business is a lot like this. What people see on the outside is the image you want to project into the world, with all of that mess hidden from view. That's fine, but it's no good pretending that mess isn't there. Business, like life, is messy and you have to deal with it one step at a time. The more you focus on improving what's happening behind the scenes in your

Introduction

business though, the fewer messes you'll have to clear up and the happier you and your team will be.

Just like life, there is also no "one size fits all" approach for a successful business. What success looks like for you will be different to what it looks like for me, or someone else who might be reading this book. Own it. I want to encourage you to be yourself, carve out your niche and stand out from the crowd.

If you've picked up this book, I imagine that you want to do things differently. You're no wall flower, you want to stand out and be noticed. This book, much like me and my business, is designed to be different to a lot of the estate agency books already out there. It's a reflection of me, my business and how I approach life; and I'm unapologetic about that. Thanks go to Gemma, one of my mentors, for that "unapologetic" phrase, which I now love. I'll come back to Gemma later on.

One thing I've learned from running my business is that you don't have to fit in and follow the crowd to be successful — challenge the status quo, and if you can see a better way of doing something, do it! This is part of developing a challenger mentality, which I'll cover in detail in Chapter 5. By sharing my experiences and story, I want to give you the confidence to

Introduction

forge your own path in the world of estate agency and residential property and build a business you can be proud of.

START WITH THE END IN MIND

One of the most important aspects of building a property business, and particularly one that challenges the status quo, is knowing what you want to achieve. As Stephen Covey says in *The 7 Habits of Highly Effective People,* "Begin with the end in mind."[1] You need to be clear about what you want to achieve, both personally and with your business. It's not for me to tell you what success looks like or even how you should go about building your business – everyone is different and what you want and how you achieve it will need to align with your values. The power comes from knowing your mission and values inside out, which is one of the first principles we'll explore in Chapter 2.

This is critical because it acts as your roadmap and only once you know where you're going can you begin putting everything else in place to make the journey as smooth as

---

1   Covey, S.R. (1997) *The Seven Habits of Highly Effective People: Restoring the Character Ethic.* Macmillan Reference USA.

Introduction

possible. The rest of the principles I'll discuss with you, such as having the right people on the bus, being a challenger, setting up efficient systems and processes, training hard and focusing on your own wellbeing and lifestyle, all rely on you knowing where you're going and what you stand for.

If you aren't interested in building an estate agency business with a strong and supportive culture at its core, that is aligned to a mission and values, stop reading now or as I like to say "change the channel honey." This book isn't for you if all you care about is making millions at any cost to your wellbeing, or that of others around you. What I've learned is that by doing the right thing, showing compassion and kindness, and staying true to your values you can build a thriving business that makes money and has a positive impact on the world. If that's the kind of business you want to create, hopefully what you'll find here are nuggets of advice to guide you on that journey and give you the support to stay the course.

LEARNING + ACTION = SUCCESS

Much of what I share in the coming chapters I have learnt from my various mentors and mastermind groups – and building

Introduction

your tribe with people who inspire you is another key foundation for long-lasting success. Again, who these people are will be different for each of you, but I know that I would not have achieved the same levels of success had I not had my mentors and peers in my corner. Not everyone who inspires you even has to be in the estate agency business— there is a lot to learn from other industries too.

My team and I are always learning, whether that's from attending courses, bringing in gurus to coach us, attending industry events in Ireland and the UK, reading books, being part of mastermind groups or looking at what others are doing for inspiration. The world is changing faster than ever before and the property business like any industry, needs to move with the times to keep up with what consumers want.

However, learning is only useful if you put what you learn into practice. You need to take consistent action and often this is what differentiates a really successful business from one that just scrapes by. Because taking purposeful and consistent action is so important, I've highlighted four key actions you can take to implement each principle at the end of each chapter. They are intended as a guide, rather than instructions, so look

Introduction

at each and see how you can implement it within your business in a way that works for you and your team.

Before we dive into the main principles I'd like to share with you though, I'd like to explain a little more about myself and Liberty Blue, and the philosophy which has been so instrumental to our success: Smarter, Faster, Better.

14

CHAPTER 1

SMARTER, FASTER, BETTER

Smarter, Faster, Better. It's a bold tagline, isn't it? I can't take credit for coming up with it, even though it perfectly describes who I am and my philosophy around business. This tagline came from our marketing consultant Paula Ronan when we were creating our brand personality and values. As soon as she said it I thought, *this is me! This is us!*

It perfectly captures my energy, and the energy in our business. This is who I am. It's who Maria, my director of almost 20 years, is. It's who everyone on the Liberty Blue team is or, should I say, needs to be. This doesn't mean we are always Smarter, Faster,

Better; but it is what we strive for. It's our roadmap. That's not to say we don't go off the road at times, but then we get right back on it.

The fact that our team also embraces the Smarter, Faster, Better mentality is important – new people start and we have to train them, coach them and show them. This takes energy, but it's hugely important. As I say to John, my manager, if the teacher doesn't show them how to do the job right, how can we blame the student? These three, simple words encompass how we approach our work and our lives. But what do they really mean? Let me begin by sharing what Smarter, Faster, Better means to me and the rest of my team.

SMARTER

Smarter is all about thinking smarter and finding ways of seeing around the corner. Trying to do things in a better way is smart. Embracing technology is smart. Using systems and processes that work is smart. All of this helps us – and can help you – to work smarter, not harder. None of us want to be busy fools. I know I don't and I'm sure if you're reading this book that you don't want to fall into that category either.

Chapter 1: Smarter, Faster, Better

Technology has played a key role in our work to become smarter in recent years. Within the business, we've introduced various pieces of technology that make us more efficient, improve our processes and systems, and allow us to provide a better service for our customers.

That said, even with technology, systems and processes in place you have to check how the team is using them. I must admit, I don't attend the team meetings often enough, but while my manager John was on holiday I recently joined one of them, which was held from our office via Zoom as we have two team members based in South Africa alongside our Waterford-based team. During that meeting I was shocked to learn that one of our team was replying to all the daft email enquiries we receive for our rental properties each day (and we can get hundreds!).

I asked why we weren't using the auto reply we have set up, which is when we discovered that the team member in question didn't know about the auto reply – it seemed it had disappeared when the person previously in that role left the business. What did I learn from this meeting? That a lot of time was going into wasteful activities that I had assumed we were doing differently. The point is that you can't get too cocky with your systems and processes – you need to drill down and review them, especially if you want to be Smarter, Faster, Better.

Our mentor Tony says we should always be trying to eliminate, automate or reduce – how right he is. In the situation I just described, a simple auto reply containing links and information is an automation that saves our people hours, and this is time that can be better spent.

Becoming smarter also means learning from others. I have mentors and regularly undertake training, and development, as do the rest of my team, to help us think smarter. This is a mindset, one that embraces innovation and doesn't stand still. It's a mantra within my business, and part of my job as the founder is to help educate everyone who works for and with us about what this mindset is and how they can develop it.

FASTER

Part of our brand personality is that we are energetic. We work at a fast pace – Maria and I both embody this. The estate agency world can be a fast-paced environment, but working faster isn't just about the speed with which you operate. It's also

Chapter 1: Smarter, Faster, Better

about being out in front and getting ahead in your industry. This is where faster complements smarter, because when you innovate you tend to push yourself ahead of your competitors.

A great example of how we got ahead of the curve is how we started seeking Google reviews from our clients and actively using social media, particularly to share videos of properties, before everyone else was doing it. This meant, among other things, that when the Covid-19 pandemic hit in 2020, we could hit the ground running. We already had the technology, systems and processes in place to enable us to work fully remotely.

But working faster also means working more efficiently, again using technology to support us. I laugh now when I think how wasteful it was that people used to have to come into our office to sign a contract or report a maintenance issue at a property. Then there would be all the follow-up emails and phone calls. So much time and energy, both on our side and our clients', was wasted by an inefficient process. Our office was so noisy; there were always people coming and going, and the phones never stopped ringing – I'm sure you can picture the scene.

Now we have technology in place that allows people to sign contracts virtually and provide all of their personal details via a secure portal. We also have a system, Fixflo, that allows tenants to report maintenance issues 24/7 without the need to come into our office or call us. We can manage our contractors through this portal, and update the tenants and owners too. This not only makes us more efficient, but also means that issues get dealt with more quickly too. It's made us faster in more ways than one.

This works really well, but I'd like to come back to the point that we need to check our systems and understand how the team is using them. In the same team meeting I mentioned earlier, I learnt that our superstar in South Africa, who runs our maintenance division, calls and emails the people who don't like to report their maintenance issues on Fixflo. I reiterated to Verisha that she can't work like that – we have a system and unless the person is elderly or has special needs then they have to log their maintenance on the online system, because otherwise she's unnecessarily adding hours to her day and we've moved away from an automated system and back to a manual one. It doesn't make sense.

Chapter 1: Smarter, Faster, Better

Whilst Verisha was doing her best to be helpful, she wasn't serving herself or the business well in terms of client management and time management. I find role-playing very helpful, so after the meeting Verisha and I role-played various scenarios where the tenant refused to log the maintenance issue online and, hey presto, Verisha saw things differently. On a call a few days later, she told me she has saved loads of time now that she is getting those few people to report online by explaining why we have this system – namely that if the tenant doesn't report the issue online, our contractor won't see it logged and it will delay how quickly we can respond, as well as limit our ability to follow up effectively. If I've learned anything in business, communication is so important and it is how we communicate that makes a huge difference. I read that from the very beginnings of military warfare, communication often holds the keys to victory.[2]

---

2   I read this at the National Museum of the Marine Corps

BETTER

Better doesn't mean we believe we're better than everyone else, but that we're always striving to be better ourselves. Personally I always want to be better than I was last year and I want the same for my business. The way to get better is to learn and innovate. Better is all about that drive to constantly find ways to improve the customer experience.

We also surround ourselves with people who share that mindset of wanting to be better, whether it's the solicitors we deal with or the contractors who maintain our clients' properties.

The only way to know if you are getting better is to audit and measure what you do – and sometimes when you carry out an audit you discover not everything is as it should be. I've even hired someone into the business whose job is to carry out weekly audits of our work. This helps keep us all accountable and ensures that we are all focused on providing the best possible customer service all the time. This lady, Debbie, is based in the UK and is highly regarded in the industry. I met Debbie at a proptech event in London and we stayed in touch – isn't it amazing that someone in another country can support your team when you have the right technology?

Chapter 1: Smarter, Faster, Better

THE POWER OF CONSISTENCY

Consistency is the key when it comes to being better, whether that's better than you were a week ago, or better than your competitors. Consistency is also part of the mantra within the business – we consistently produce agent-led property videos; we consistently host our Live After 5s on social media containing tips and property updates; we consistently run expert webinars; and we consistently send out our monthly Waterford Property Watch newsletter. This level of consistency has been instrumental in our success and is one of the reasons we are the highest five-star Google reviewed estate agency in Ireland (at the time of writing this book).

You have to put the hard grind in. In many ways, building a successful business is a lot like becoming physically fitter and stronger. If you want those muscles, you know you've got to go to the gym at least three times a week, follow your programme and make sure you're eating the right levels of protein and other nutrients. You need to do this consistently to see results. You need to carve out time for your gym sessions and meal prep. It's no different when you're running a business.

However, the challenge when you're running a business is that you get sucked into the day-to-day "doing" and that prevents you from being able to work on the long-term strategy. You have to be ruthless and carve out time to work on your strategy and you have to do so consistently. One of the things that will help you make that time is having the right team around you – or the right people on the bus – and communicating clearly with them.

The principles I'm going to share with you throughout the coming chapters are a recipe for building a sustainable business that can grow and thrive, provided you follow them consistently.

FOCUS ON THE SMALL DETAILS

Our tagline of Smarter, Faster, Better, encompasses the energy myself, my director Maria Clifford and our business exudes. It also speaks to the can-do attitude we have and our desire to go the extra mile for all of our clients. The difference between ordinary and extraordinary is "extra", so our philosophy is about doing extra and anticipating people's needs.

Chapter 1: Smarter, Faster, Better

For example, when someone sends an email, don't just send them the bare bones of an answer – give them additional information so that they don't have to come back to you with another question. When you put yourself in the shoes of the customer, or the person asking the question, and you give them extra you create moments of delight. That's what Smarter, Faster, Better is all about. Extra doesn't have to be anything huge. In fact, it's often the small details that make all the difference.

I know, as a consumer, that it's the small, thoughtful details that will impress me far more than the bigger things. For example, if I go to the restaurant that I like to eat at in Dungarvan, and the manager Mike greets me with "Regina, I've got your usual table over here. Can I get you a glass of red wine?" I feel delighted. Mike is anticipating my needs and giving me extra. The point is, creating moments of delight often doesn't take a lot, but it makes a huge difference to someone's experience of your business and the service you provide.

The example I just shared is about a place I regularly visit, but I believe service should always be this smooth. If I go somewhere new, they may not know my drink order, but they can welcome me in, seat me at my table with a menu and get me a drink in those first five to ten minutes, and then I'll relax. If it takes too long for someone to take my drink order or bring me a menu, I get irritated and it tarnishes the whole experience. You only have a short period in which to create that positive first impression. This is why I insist that, whenever someone comes into the office, one of the team stands up, greets them and asks how they can help as soon as they're through the door.

In any business, you have to do the big things well – that's expected – but it's the little extras that will make your business stand out. Those are what will make your clients consider you to be better than your competition, and that's true in any industry, not just estate agencies.

Lighting the fire

Years ago I ran my own event management business. In the early '90s I was responsible for the PR of a musical, which I'd convinced film director Jim Sheridan to attend. He even cancelled a holiday in France to be there. He was coming with his wife Fran and agreed to review the show – it was a big deal to have this famous Irish film director visiting Waterford.

Chapter 1: Smarter, Faster, Better

I wanted everything about his stay to be perfect. We arranged beautiful accommodation for him and his wife, I put food and drink in the fridge and provided flowers. On the morning of their arrival, only one thing was missing...

I turned to my friend Billy who was helping with the organisation of the event. "We need to get some firelighters and matches in case they want to light the fire." He laughed, "Don't be ridiculous! Just forget about it, they aren't going to have time to light the fire." After protesting, I eventually agreed. Billy was probably right, they had a pretty full schedule...

Jim and his wife arrived, and the show was brilliant. They met with the writer Brian Fynn (who has since passed away, RIP) and discussed bringing the show to Broadway. It didn't work out, but it was an exciting opportunity. When Jim was leaving, I asked how his stay was. His reply has always stayed with me: "It was amazing. We loved the accommodation and everything you did, it was just a pity we couldn't light the fire."

That was when I vowed that, even if other people thought I was stressing over something small, if it could be done I'd make sure it was.

My team will tell you that I'm very calm when someone gets a big thing wrong, but I go mad when the small details aren't taken care of. I've always believed that if customers think you can't look after the small things, they'll also question how you're going to look after the big things. This focus on getting the details right pays off.

I remember coming into the office one morning ahead of a visit by some VIP clients to find the windows looked dirty. One of my team told me that the cleaners had been the day before, so they must have got dirty in the rain overnight. I didn't care that the windows had been cleaned the day before, because they weren't clean now, so I called the contractor and insisted they send someone over to clean the windows again. Long story short, the windows were spotless by the time our VIP clients showed up.

What was the first thing the clients did? That's right, looked through the window. Now, I'm sure the clean windows weren't the only reason they did, and still do, business with us. But the clean windows were part of making that strong first impression. We have been doing business with these clients for 11 years now.

Chapter 1: Smarter, Faster, Better

This focus on the small details is one of the reasons I believe our business has been so successful. One of the other elements that has played into our success is our adoption of technology.

INNOVATE TO IMPROVE

Technology has played a huge role in making our business Smarter, Faster, Better. In 2015, I decided Maria and I should attend a proptech conference in London. I organised the trip and said to her, "We don't know what we don't know, we need to go to this event." At this stage in our business journey, we didn't have a clue what technology was available for the property industry and we didn't know where to start with introducing it either. This trip to London changed everything – we learnt so much and met some amazing people who helped us significantly improve our business efficiency. One of those people was Kristjan Byfield.

Kristjan gave a talk at the conference. He stood out for two reasons – firstly, his passion for what he was doing really impressed me and, secondly, he looked like a Viking. I was blown away by Kristjan; he was so smart and talked about the systems they used in his business – Base in London. It was light years ahead of ours. After his speech, I introduced myself and Maria, and asked if we could visit his business as it sounded amazing. He agreed. Little did he realise that I'd be on the phone to him within a few days arranging all of this and that, just ten days later, I'd be in his London office with three of my team!

None of this phased him though. Kristjan was incredibly generous with his time. He and his team gave us a whole day of gold. We listened, asked a lot of questions and I left with a very clear idea of what our business needed to look like in the future. I had a vision from that day that I was going to make come true.

What struck me most about his office was how quiet it was. It was calm, the phone rarely rang and nobody other than staff came in or out on the day we were there. It was the polar opposite of our office at the time, which was always jammed with people, had phones constantly ringing and had an underlying sense of stress.

In the four years after that visit to Kristjan's office, we implemented 14 new pieces of technology and this has transformed our business. I mentioned the Fixflo software for reporting and managing maintenance issues earlier, but other software included PlanetVerify, which allows tenants to upload their

Chapter 1: Smarter, Faster, Better

data in a secure and efficient way. What's more, it's all securely stored in the cloud and anyone on our team can access it if need be. It's quite a contrast to how we operated before, where all tenants had to email their references and documentation to one person in the office – finding paperwork was like searching for a needle in a haystack and God forbid the person in charge of references was off sick for even a day! Does that sound familiar?

These two pieces of software are just some of the reasons why, when the Covid-19 pandemic hit, we were able to largely continue with business as usual. In fact, we rented over 60 properties during the pandemic without meeting anyone in person. Where we had to change our processes, we innovated. For instance, we got our cleaners to shoot videos of the properties on their phones when they were doing their jobs, as they were still allowed to go to properties whereas agents were not. That meant we could still share video walkthroughs of all the properties on our books, despite our team all working from home.

PUT IN THE FLYING HOURS TO SUCCEED

Success doesn't come overnight, even when it looks to the outside world like it might have. Much like learning to fly a plane, you have to put in the flying hours. We have spent years developing our systems, improving the way in which we operate and innovating in areas such as marketing. This means we've had a lot of practice and that's enabling us to take on much larger projects than we have in the past. As I mentioned earlier, you also need to continuously check these wonderful systems to ensure everyone is using them the way they are meant to be used, rather than deviating from them and creating more work.

Our videos are one of our biggest selling points, and they work incredibly well in our marketing, but we have spent years honing and sharpening our video skills. We look at what other agents in the UK and beyond do to get inspiration, we go on training courses, and we have practised a lot. Consistency is key. When preparation like this meets opportunity, your business soars to new heights. Our videos are one of our unique selling points (USPs), and a point of difference from our competitors. So, if you aren't doing videos you need to start, now!

Chapter 1: Smarter, Faster, Better

I consider building a business the same as learning to drive a car. I vividly remember how challenging learning to drive a car was. I bought my first car – a banger of a Toyota Starlet – after waiting for hours at the bus stop only for the bus to never arrive. I had my provisional licence and I drove all the way to my parents' house – a four hour round trip – in third gear, and spent most of my time wondering why the hell my car sounded so terrible!

I hadn't had anywhere near enough practice to do that drive. But the more hours I spent in the car, the more I learnt about how it worked (and that I needed to shift out of third gear!).

To learn to drive, you need to have the right instructor, so for a business these are your mentors. You need to have the right people around you to support you, who are your mastermind group. You need to make sure you know what good looks like and constantly educate yourself on changes within your industry. Part of this involves working out how you can incorporate what you learn into your business in a way that suits your style and market. And you need to put in the hours. You can't pass a driving test after just a couple of hours at the wheel, you have to practise until it becomes second nature. Building a successful business is no different.

But practice, while important, isn't the whole story. You also need to be prepared to get out of your comfort zone. I have delivered hundreds of hours of videos for our business to date, as well as having been on primetime TV, but I'm not always comfortable in front of a camera, even now. I prepare a lot, especially if it's a media appearance, but more importantly I have become comfortable with being uncomfortable.

This is the key – I have accepted that not everything I have to do to grow my business is in my comfort zone, but I know that even if it makes me feel uncomfortable at the time, it's worth it in the long run. The second element of this is maximising the opportunities you create by pushing yourself out of your comfort zone.

Our mission as a business is to be helpful experts, and to champion Waterford as a great place to live. Producing video content is all part of that mission, and that makes it much easier for me to find the courage to push myself out of my comfort zone.

If you're reading this book, I'm going to hazard a guess that you're not afraid to stand out. As we move through the coming chapters, I'm going to help you develop the mindset you need

Chapter 1: Smarter, Faster, Better

to stand out from the crowd and stand by your convictions. Not everyone will love what you do or how you do it, and that's OK. Sometimes you need faith to keep doing what you're doing, because it will get you the results you're looking for.

STAYING THE COURSE

My hope is that this book will provide you with the encouragement and inspiration to stand out from the crowd and stay true to who you are, even in the face of criticism. I also hope that my story will encourage you to keep plugging away, to put in those flying hours, knowing that even if you have a bumpy ride at the start it will get smoother the more you practise.

Business isn't a smooth ride – I'm not going to sugarcoat things, you will have some really bad days (I know I have). But for every difficult day there will be many more amazing ones and sometimes you just have to get your head down, keep doing what you do best and remember to shift gears.

As a business owner in the 2020s, you have a world of opportunities open to you that simply weren't there when I started out – people still sent messages by fax and Telex in the early days of my business, now we have multiple social media platforms and so many more opportunities to share our message, show people who we are and make connections.

In a world where there are so many messages and so many ways to reach people, without knowing who you are and what you stand for, you don't really have a chance of standing out. How can you communicate what makes you uniquely "you" to the rest of the world if you're not clear on this yourself?

That's why we need to make sure your values and mission are straight first, because they form the foundations for your business.

CHAPTER 2

VALUES AND MISSION

Before we explore how you can use your values and mission within your business, it's important to understand the difference between the two. For me, our mission is what we strive to achieve every day and our values are how we achieve it.

Our mission at Liberty Blue is to *bring happiness to our customers, colleagues and community, and to be helpful experts and champions of Waterford, showcasing that it is a great place to live.*

Your mission is like the roadmap for your business, and your values are the compass that help ensure you stick to that roadmap. Without knowing your mission and values, you won't know why you're showing up everyday and, if you are just chasing money, you could find that what you're doing is in conflict with your values, even if you don't consciously realise it at the time.

Having clarity over your mission and values brings you and your business many benefits. Firstly, it allows you to have much more productive conversations both within your team and with clients or prospective clients. Secondly, it makes decisions much easier, because you can ask yourself whether taking a certain action will help you achieve your mission and whether it aligns with your values – whether the answer to both of those questions is "yes" or "no", it's an easy decision. It's rare you'll answer "no" to one, but "yes" to the other.

For example, part of our mission is to be champions of Waterford and bring happiness to our community. While I was writing this book, we were approached about cosponsoring the Waterford News & Star Green Room Awards, which celebrate Waterford's theatre, arts and cultural scene. Cosponsoring the awards was an obvious choice for us – we can't say that our mission is to bring happiness to our community and then not back it up.

The night of the awards, Maria and I felt insanely proud. We presented about 15 awards between us and it was one of the

Chapter 2: Values and Mission

best things we've ever done. We measured the success of our sponsorship by the levels of happiness in that room and it was an amazing opportunity to be in a room with people from our community who we may not meet on a day-to-day basis. Of course, our branding was on the stage as a cosponsor, which was an opportunity to showcase our business to even more people.

As another example of how our mission guides our actions and business decisions, we send clients chocolates made in Waterford as gifts. When we were choosing what to gift, the decision became very easy once we focused on our mission and values. Even though a box of these locally made chocolates is more expensive than some of the other options we considered, it ties in perfectly with our mission of bringing happiness to those we work with and being Waterford experts who support their local community.

LIVING YOUR VALUES

Many of the values that we live by within the business are values I developed growing up on the family farm. I remember my mother often talked about respect and doing the right thing.

She taught me the importance of being respectful, not only to other people, but also to myself. These values have always been part of Liberty Blue, but it wasn't until 2020 that we discussed the business' values as a team.

Through this discussion, we agreed the main values we live and work by at Liberty Blue are:

- » We do the right thing
- » We take pride in everything we do
- » We love to innovate

Since documenting our values, we've become conscious of the role they play in many areas of the business, from how we treat our clients to who we hire. In fact, hiring on values is hugely important, because you can teach someone the job, but you can't teach them the right attitude – this is something I'll come back to in Chapter 3.

Defining our values as a business also gives me confidence that, even when I'm not in the room, my team will know how to behave in any situation and will behave in such a way that it enhances the reputation of the company.

Chapter 2: Values and Mission

So, what does living by your values look like in the real world? Let's look at some of our values to see how they guide our behaviour and how that benefits the business.

» *DO THE RIGHT THING*

A number of years ago, we fired a client. We managed over 50 properties for him, but he didn't behave in the right way and look after his tenants. This client was a real bully – towards our staff and his tenants. It was really stressful dealing with him and his team. He would do things like demand we change locks and refuse to maintain the properties.

We made the decision to fire this client not long after the 2008 financial crash, even though he would have brought the business a significant amount of annual revenue. But the client didn't want to maintain his properties to a good standard, he didn't want to fix anything that went wrong – even when the locks broke! We decided to take a hit in our income because we knew that this client wasn't aligned with our values, in fact we were miles apart in terms of how we behave.

Financially that could have been a difficult decision, but even though it meant lost income for the business, the choice to step away from that client was a very straightforward one. You can't do the right thing just 80 per cent of the time when it's easy; you have to do the right thing *all* the time, even if it hurts, because that's how you live by your values and demonstrate your integrity.

Doing the right thing can also mean giving people, including clients, uncomfortable feedback. I recently had a vendor who called me in the middle of the night (I didn't answer, but I had multiple missed calls on a Sunday morning!) – I knew then that the right thing to do was tell her, politely but firmly, that we couldn't sell her property for her. It would have been too stressful for my team and I.

There was a time when I would have wanted to sell this woman's property, just to prove I could get the results she was looking for. Now, however, clearly guided by our company values, I knew it wouldn't be the right thing to do for my team, so I let her go as a client.

» ALWAYS TELL THE TRUTH – BECAUSE WE DO THE RIGHT THING

This is a big one in the world of property, where there are generally low levels of trust among the public for the profession – but

Chapter 2: Values and Mission

trust is everything. We are upfront about all the properties we sell or rent and are honest about any issues they have. I once valued a property where the septic tank didn't work and the owner asked if we should tell prospective buyers about the issue.

I was adamant that we should tell the truth and be upfront about it, even though another agent had suggested that the seller just not mention it to any potential buyers. For me, not saying anything wasn't even a consideration, because I'd have been omitting an important truth from the listing and it's not the right thing to do. In my experience, when you're selling a property and you're upfront about any problems it has, the trust level that a buyer has in you shoots way up, so it is actually beneficial in many ways.

We will also hold our hands up and tell our clients if we were wrong or if we've screwed up. We apologise, explain what we're doing to ensure the same issue doesn't happen again and we move forward. Learning from our mistakes is how we become better, but we also have to acknowledge them and apologise when they impact others.

» *RESPECT – DO THE RIGHT THING*

We expect everyone we work with, clients and colleagues alike, to be respectful towards us and we will always do the same. This one also closely links with *do the right thing*, because if someone is being disrespectful, or in some cases abusive, towards my team then clearly the right thing to do is to pull them up on it, and if it is a continuous problem then we decide how to address the problem – through a meeting or if necessary by firing them.

We once had a landlord come into our office screaming and roaring over something incredibly trivial (I think one of his tenants had left a McDonald's wrapper on the table when they moved out). He was being erratic and abusive. There was no reasoning with him. I told him that we wouldn't be looking after his three properties any more. It's important to mention it wasn't his first rodeo of very bad behaviour.

He wasn't respecting me or my team, so the decision was easy. It's incredibly important to protect your team's energy and mental health. If you allow people to be abusive, then none of you will flourish, and neither will your business.

Chapter 2: Values and Mission

Sometimes when you point out unacceptable or disrespectful behaviour, people can change their approach. We had one lady who used to send emails in red, capital letters with sentences underlined – Miriam, who has been on the team for 15 years, told me she found these emails very offensive, so I called the client and explained that the way she communicated via email was upsetting my team members. I told her that I would be happy to give her the keys back to the houses we managed for her, and that she could do business with someone else.

She didn't apologise, but she practically pleaded with me not to send her keys back. I put her on a trial period and made it very clear that if her communication became offensive again, we'd stop working with her. I also stressed that my team always tries to do the best they can for every one of our clients, but there are no guarantees that everything will always be perfect. She hasn't sent an email in capital letters, red text or with multiple points underlined, since. By standing up for my team, and ensuring all our clients respect their efforts, I'm living by both my and the business' values.

I don't want you to think that I constantly have to fire clients – these are very isolated incidents – but dealing with them is made a lot easier with the compass of our business values to

45

guide me. There is no question about continuing to work with people like this for the sake of money – their behaviour isn't acceptable, and if they don't change when I call them out then it's clear their values aren't aligned with ours and that it's best if we part ways.

THE BENEFITS OF BEING EXPLICIT ABOUT YOUR VALUES

Prior to 2020, we lived by these values within the business, but we hadn't explicitly identified and shared them with the rest of the team. Now that we are all very clear about what our company values are, it's made decision making much quicker – we've become faster – and knowing our values has enabled us to set clear boundaries, making life better for all of us.

Over the years, several of my mentors have helped me see the importance of setting out values within our business – John Paul, Matt Giggs and Gemma Noonan (who works for Matt), all come to mind. I remember one conversation with Gemma in particular, when she was talking about how to use your values when engaging with your people, as well as when you're engaging with your clients. She asked, "Regina, what's the right

Chapter 2: Values and Mission

thing to do when someone screws up? Is it to pick them up on every mistake they make, or to have a one-on-one conversation to discuss the mistake and keep them motivated?"

I'm not saying I picked on people over every mistake, but that simple question made me realise how important the happiness of our people is and it clearly focused us on the fact that part of our mission is to bring happiness to our colleagues, as well as to our clients and community. It helped us to examine the ways we'd been managing people to date, and showed us how we could change to manage in a way that made everyone happier.

We identified our values by working with our marketing consultant Paula, and I would strongly recommend that you work with an external consultant to identify the values within your own business and team. Often when you're in the weeds, it's harder to see what your values really are.

You also need to ensure that there's buy-in for your company values from all stakeholders, whoever they are, although usually this will mean your team. As a business owner, it's important that you don't come up with the company values and impose them on your team – there needs to be some healthy debate about what you all value and stand for together, because this is how you'll get buy-in for those values from the whole team.

REFINING AND LIVING YOUR MISSION STATEMENT

Your mission statement will be closely connected to your values, but again, it's something that you should discuss with your whole team to get buy-in. Our mission statement of bringing happiness to our customers and colleagues might sound a little intangible, but we believe that if our colleagues are inspired and happy, they'll do their best work which will benefit both the business and our customers.

There are various ways in which we bring happiness to our staff, from organising wellness days and taking them out for team lunches, to renovating our office. The office renovation has made a much bigger difference than you may think to the happiness of our team, because it feels like a much cooler space to work in – it's completely changed the atmosphere of the office.

Since renovating the office, we've introduced morning team meetings, which is helping everyone bond as a team and we're

Chapter 2: Values and Mission

seeing greater commitment to the business from our staff too. Even though two of our full-time team members are based in South Africa, they find the interaction from the team meetings really helps them feel part of the team. These meetings are also a great way for everyone to discuss the plan for the day, including viewings, appointments and any issues. One of my mentors in the UK, who has multiple offices, told me that his teams who meet every morning are the most successful.

We've also introduced bi-weekly one-to-ones with each member of the team, which gives everyone a chance to talk about what's going well for them, what could be going better and to ask for any help or support they need. As I'm writing this book, these regular one-to-ones are still very new for us, but we're already seeing the positive results. They have improved the levels of accountability within the team, and everyone feels that they are heard by their manager because they know they'll have that 30 or 40 minutes carved out just for them every couple of weeks.

THE POWER OF KNOWING
YOUR VALUES AND MISSION

Looking back, I can see how not having complete clarity over the values and mission of the business has led to poor decisions in the past, or in some cases relationships with clients whose values didn't align with ours carrying on for several years too long. The biggest cost of working with clients like this, in my experience, is that the work stops being enjoyable and this can have the knock-on effect of damaging your confidence.

Often managing these relationships takes up far more of your time and energy than it should and, especially as I've got older, I've come to realise that time is the most valuable commodity on the planet. You don't want to waste it with the wrong people, and you don't want your team to do that either.

Since identifying our values and mission, we talk about them with our clients and we examine our client relationships through those lenses. For example by asking questions like, how can we bring happiness to our colleagues if all the interactions they have with a particular client are negative because their values don't align with ours?

Chapter 2: Values and Mission

My manager John thanked me only yesterday for having his back. A client had really upset him. In this instance, the client was most unreasonable and sent rude and unprofessional emails about John. I advised the client that John would handle the issue and stressed that I had every confidence in him. John apologised by email and invited the client in for a coffee to try to resolve the matter, but the client didn't even respond. John knows I have full confidence in him, and he knows that I've told the client this. If this landlord wants to move their property from us, that's absolutely fine – we can do no more. For us, the happiness of our people is very important and they will be much happier when they know we have their backs.

Over the years we have definitely spent a lot of time working with some very wrong clients for us, and if I had my time over again, I wouldn't do that. When we clarified our values and mission in 2020, it made me evaluate our client relationships in this new light and I let some long-standing clients go as a result.

I resigned the business from the management of five apartment blocks because our happiness levels when dealing with these properties was incredibly low on every front. In this instance it was less to do with the client's values not being aligned with ours and more to do with the level of work that was required to manage these blocks. We had been managing these blocks for 10, or in some cases 15 years, and as a result there was a lack of clarity over the rules of engagement – there were a lot of grey areas and we ended up providing excessive levels of service for which we didn't bill.

The client's expectations weren't aligned with what we were prepared to deliver. During the Covid-19 pandemic, many of the clients that didn't truly align with us expected even more of us and it simply wasn't viable without significantly impacting the happiness levels of all of us in the business, so I let them go. I didn't tell my team at the time though, because I didn't want any of them to try and talk me out of it based on the financial implications. I knew it was the right thing to do for our mission and values, even if it seemed like we'd lose out financially.

In fact, because of the extra hours and energy we were pouring into managing these developments, we didn't make as much as we should have and, therefore, didn't lose too much when we walked away from them.

When you're new to business, the idea of turning down a pay-ing client can feel terrifying – trust me when I say I understand your fear. But what I would say, having stayed with clients who

Chapter 2: Values and Mission

don't align for years longer than we should, is that it never ends well when you compromise on your values and mission for someone else.

I also believe that when one door closes another opens. Of course the more financially comfortable you become in your business the easier those decisions get, but it's important to assess your decisions to take on new business by considering more than just money. Look at how many hours you'd spend on a client during the week – are they worth that? Are there other opportunities you could explore instead?

Being happy at work is important – I'm not saying that everything will be perfect all the time for every client, but over-all you and your clients need to be happy working together. So, ask yourself whether taking on more work that you don't really enjoy is going to serve you and make you happy.

If you do take on clients or work that aren't ideal, use your values to set very clear boundaries about the rules of engagement for your relationship with the client. Be very clear about what services you will and won't provide, and during what hours you will provide them. If a client wants services outside of these hours, be upfront about the additional charges for providing

53

them. You have to be prepared to stand your ground and stick to your boundaries, otherwise you will likely end up feeling pretty miserable.

I remember taking calls from one client between 7–8pm at night in the early days of my business. I shouldn't have answered my phone that late, but I did, and in doing so I set out the unwritten rule of engagement that this client could call me outside my normal working hours. I wasn't respectful of myself in taking calls this late and I wasn't respectful of the client either, because I sent the signal that I needed to talk to them that late too.

My advice if you're setting up a business is to be prepared to push back and set boundaries, because both you and your clients will benefit in the long run if you do.

KNOWING YOUR BRAND PERSONALITY

Setting boundaries is much easier when you have a clearly defined brand personality, as well as values and a mission. Your brand personality is slightly different to your values because it encompasses how you behave and present to the outside

Chapter 2: Values and Mission

world. The Liberty Blue brand personality is that we're straight talking, intelligent and empathetic. I can use this to frame my interactions with my clients.

Using the Liberty Blue brand personality, I might start out by saying, "I'm delighted to have this contract with you and I think we're going to do very well, but I'd just like to start our relationship by talking about how I do business. My team and I are available until 5.30pm Monday to Friday, and every second Saturday from 10–11am. If there's an issue, I'm going to be very direct with you about it. Are you OK with that?"

If the client's response is, "No, I'm not OK with that. To be honest I don't like people who are direct and I'd prefer it if you kept your thoughts to yourself," I would question whether this is a right-fit client for us. I know that to give the best of myself, I need to be direct, so maybe this client isn't right for the business and I should let them go.

Having this clarity won't always feel comfortable, in fact it will often feel uncomfortable, but as I said in the first chapter, it's important to become comfortable with being uncomfortable and having those uncomfortable conversations. This is why, again, knowing your values and mission is so important, because it gives you the confidence to stand up for what's right for you and your team, and makes it easier for you to communicate your boundaries to clients.

As a business owner, you can't escape uncomfortable conversations, whether they're with clients, staff, business associates or neighbours. You have to deal with poor behaviour and stand up for yourself, otherwise you'll become a slave to everyone. When you start a business, it can feel difficult to have this level of confidence when you need to make money, but take a moment to consider what your values protect – they protect your mental and physical health. You need to keep both these in check if you're going to succeed, so although it can be difficult, try to make money just one of the factors you consider in your decision, not the whole of it.

Think about it this way, if you are working with clients who aren't engaging in a way that works for you, it's going to cause havoc with your mental health and wellbeing. When you are stressed and unhappy, you will be absolutely useless for the rest of your clients and it will have a negative effect on your personal life too. You can't give your power away for financial gain which, when you factor in the cost of your time and energy, almost certainly won't be worth it.

Chapter 2: Values and Mission

This doesn't mean you have to turn away clients who aren't exactly aligned with your values, simply that you have to set clear boundaries from the outset so that you keep your power. When you support your boundaries with your values, it enables you to have this conversation in a way that is respectful of the other person too, and that helps them understand how to work with you in a way that's positive for both of you.

HOW TO SHARE YOUR VALUES, MISSION AND BRAND PERSONALITY

When it comes to sharing your values and mission with your team, I've certainly found it's beneficial to have them somewhere visible in your office. Our mission is on the wall in our meeting room, and our values are displayed in reception to remind everyone, including our clients, what we stand for.

We also refer to our values and mission during our morning meetings. This is a good way to frame the conversation and, again, just remind everyone what we're doing and why. Having this visibility of our values and mission also sets the tone for doing business.

Remember that the starting point for your values is what's important to you. When you start your own business this will be natural to you, but it's important that you go through the process of identifying your business values and learn how to communicate those clearly with others, because it sets you up for even greater success when you do. It is particularly important when you start recruiting.

Chapter 2: Values and Mission

Steps for success

- Know your mission – this is your roadmap to keep everyone on track as the business grows.

- Live your values – agree your values with your team, and they'll live by them too.

- Set boundaries – when you know your mission and what you value, you can set boundaries that support you and your team.

- Share who you are – don't keep your mission and values to yourself, share them with clients, contractors and the wider world.

We have to remind ourselves of our values and our mission. I regularly put a picture of our mission, vision, values and personality into our team WhatsApp group and ask them to comment. These are things that I need to remind the team of and that we have to discuss regularly in order for us to really and honestly live them. In other words, it's always a work in progress.

CHAPTER 3

HAVE THE RIGHT PEOPLE ON THE BUS

In 1995, I got on a bus to travel from Dublin to Waterford. That bus journey changed my life. All I knew when I climbed on and took my seat was that I was travelling to Waterford to start my new job running an aparthotel, the Adelphi Wharf Suites. I'd never been to Waterford before, but I was clear about the destination.

A few months earlier, I'd been introduced to Jim Murphy, who was setting up the aparthotel I was now going to be managing. When I met Jim, I was working at a hotel in Bray and I hated it. Not only that, but my personal living situation was terrible –

Chapter 3: Have the Right People on the Bus

I was living with a woman I didn't get on with who seemed to delight in making me miserable. I was looking for a way to escape this unfulfilling life in Bray.

When Jim asked to interview me for the job at an aparthotel he was responsible for in Waterford, I jumped at the chance. So, that's how I came to be sitting on a bus bound for Waterford on Good Friday 1995. I was ready to leave Bray behind and move on with my life.

The journey to Waterford takes a little over two hours from Dublin and as we travelled, people hopped on and off the bus. There was a constantly changing set of characters on the vehicle throughout the journey.

WHAT DOES A BUS HAVE TO DO WITH BUSINESS?

I was introduced to the concept of having the right people on the bus by several of my business mentors, including Sanjay Gandhi (the founder of Moss Mentors, not the famous politician!) and John Paul, but it stems from Jim Collins' book *Good to Great*.[3]

For me, having the right people on the bus has several layers of meaning. The bus is your business, but it really all starts with the driver of the bus, who is the leader of the business (me or you in this case). The driver needs to know where the bus is going and they need to communicate that with everyone else who's sitting on the bus. This is all about having clarity over your vision and mission, as well as knowing what you need to get there. On a long bus journey, you'll need food, water, repair kits and so on to sustain not only the people on the bus, but the bus itself.

Within a business, this is about developing the capacity within your workplace to deliver the work to your clients. You need to give the people on your team appropriate training and access to the right resources, so that they have the confidence to do their job well and clarity over what their role is.

---

3 Collins, J.J. (2001) *Good to Great*. Available at: https://e-library.ittelkom-jkt. ac.id/index.php?p=show_detail&id=89.

Chapter 3: Have the Right People on the Bus

Not everyone who starts our bus ride with us will go the distance. Just like people were coming and going on my bus journey from Dublin to Waterford, sometimes in business people will leave. Some of those will press the bell and voluntarily get off the bus, others will require you to pull over and ask them to leave at the next stop. My bus journey has lasted 26 years so far – and there have been a lot of people jumping on and off in that time!

Over the years I've also been involved in maintaining the bus and doing all manner of jobs, from fixing the tyres and replacing headlight bulbs, to cleaning the bus and repairing the upholstery on the seats! My mentor Sanjay often says, "The pilot doesn't serve the drinks" – it's not different on a bus, in that the driver shouldn't be serving the drinks (or doing all the maintenance and cleaning) either. You need a team to help with all of those other jobs.

The driver is supposed to drive the bus, keeping one eye on the road ahead and making sure that we're all moving in the right direction. Driving the bus is an analogy for taking care of the strategic direction of your business. This is when you're working *on* the business, rather than *in* the business.

While you shouldn't be doing all the maintenance and repair work yourself as the bus driver, it is still helpful to do this sometimes. In a business, it helps you stay in touch with what's happening on the ground and that can help you make better strategic decisions. So, if you know you're going to need to put more fuel in the bus' tank soon, you'll stick to the main roads where you're more likely to pass a petrol station, rather than taking country lanes and risking running out of fuel before you reach your next stop.

When I first started writing this book, I would say I was spending about half my time working on the business and half my time working in it, which was a good place to be because it enabled me to be more strategic and work on the "important but not urgent" tasks. This is a vital distinction, because it's the important, rather than the urgent, tasks that will get you to your destination – or in other words help you realise your vision and mission in the business. My focus was on the growth and development of my people and my business – I can't do any of that if I'm showing houses from 9am to 6pm every day, but I still need to know how these tasks are carried out to help me make strategic adjustments and set up the right training plans for everyone else.

Chapter 3: Have the Right People on the Bus

However, eight months on, as I'm getting closer to finishing this book, this has changed because a key person in the business is on leave for a few months – which is completely necessary, and it's important to support your A team when they need it. As they say, the best laid plans and all that! This does mean I've gone from having about half my time working on the business to being fully immersed in the day-to-day of the business again. Whilst it can be a little stressful to be driving the bus, fixing the wheels and a whole lot more, I am using it as an opportunity to sharpen the saw. I'm more involved in viewings, valuations and the day-to-day interactions within our operation.

In the three months that I've been back in the day-to-day, I've learnt that you need to check the processes to make sure they're being used correctly (remember my story about my team member who was deviating from our process for reporting maintenance issues in an attempt to be helpful to clients?). The key to processes being followed is clarity – for the team to understand why we have a system, how to deal with objections from clients, how to sell it to them, and the benefits to everyone as a result of using our systems consistently and correctly. They need training and as a business leader, it's our job to provide that training.

I've been pushing the whole team to make more client calls and check in with them to see if there's anything else we can do to help. I asked everyone on the team to step up and when they have a problem I'm coaching them on how to find the answers for themselves.

Coaching is an important part of being the bus driver – you need coaching from your mentors and you need to provide coaching to your team. When you do, they can thrive. One team member in lettings and viewings has flourished since I started coaching him more. He isn't keen on delegating tasks, but I have convinced him that by delegating such tasks as advert writing to a more junior member of the team, he can save time that he can then use to help me. He loves the challenge and, what's even better is that the team member he's delegated that task to is not only particularly good at writing adverts, but is also using AI to speed up the process. When everyone is learning more, you can leverage more. As my mentor Tony says, "Let no dilemma or crisis in a business go to waste."

As I write this, I'm also coaching and mentoring Darragh, who's working on our social media content. This used to be part of my role, so as I'm handing it over to him we're working closely together so he knows what good looks like. Once he's fully

Chapter 3: Have the Right People on the Bus

trained, I'll be able to leave him in his seat and trust that his part of our "bus" will be well maintained and continue to bring in new clients. The other side to this is that Darragh loves this part of the job and we need to create an environment where people grow and thrive. That's how we keep talent.

WHO CAN GET ON YOUR BUS?

Often when people talk about having the right people on their bus, they limit this to employees, but in the early years of a business the chances are you won't have many employees because money is tight – for many years I had just one full-time employee and we were working hand-to-mouth to pay both her and myself. It was only once the business grew substantially that I was able to hire more people. But, that doesn't mean that for those first six years it was just Sinead and I on the bus – many other seats were occupied, they just weren't my direct employees. Nora, my bank manager, is a good example of someone who's been pivotal to the business' success, but has never worked for me.

Bringing Nora onboard

When I arrived in Waterford, I settled straight into work. One of the people I met through working at the aparthotel was Nora, who was the bank manager for the business. We developed a good relationship and I respected and liked her, so when I decided to start my own business two years after moving to Waterford, she was someone I wanted on my "bus".

I also had a business partner, Peter, for the first year. Whilst it didn't work out, it ended amicably and I might not have done it on my own – I was really young and clueless, but I guess brave, looking back. So, my business partner Peter and I needed a loan of £10,000 to get the business off the ground. I put together a business plan and feasibility study, as well as forecasts and projections. In all honesty it felt like I was trying to predict the following week's Lotto numbers as I didn't know what these kinds of documents should look like, but I did the best I could with what I knew at the time, and I presented my plan and figures to Nora. When I finished she thanked me and as I left the room I knew she wasn't going to give me the money. I took a deep breath, turned around, knocked on the door and walked back in.

Chapter 3: Have the Right People on the Bus

"Nora, I just wanted to let you know that you've got 24 hours to make up your mind because my business partner Peter wants to give our business to the other bank, but I told him I really only wanted to do business with you, so I'll leave it with you."

This time, Nora stood and thanked me profusely. As I left her office for the second time that morning, I felt a lot more confident. Sure enough, the following day she called to give us the £10,000 we needed. This was the beginning of a very long working relationship with Nora, and it's one that has been very important to me and my business. Nora had a prime seat on my bus, and I'll tell you why.

About five years into the business, I ran into some really tough times. I was in Dublin trying to secure a big contract for the company when Nora phoned me. "Regina, there are a lot of cheques that are going to bounce this week because you don't have enough money in the bank."

"I'm in Dublin working to secure a contract – you can't bounce those cheques."

"Well how are you going to pay?"

69

"Trust me, I'm going to win this contract and then I'll have a steady income, but if you bounce those cheques it'll be the end of the business and the end of me, and there will be no money going back to the bank. I need you to stick with me. I'll call you in 48 hours."

Nora agreed. She trusted me, she believed in me and she went out on a limb when things were looking very, very sticky. But I can honestly say that if it wasn't for Nora, I probably wouldn't be in business today. I also made sure that I kept my side of the agreement – I called her when I said I would and I kept the lines of communication between us open.

This continued, not only in relation to this specific contract, but going forward. I reported to her regularly, telling her what I was doing to bring in new business. She could see I was a hard worker and she knew I'd do what I said I would – this built a strong, trusting relationship. Even though Nora was supportive, I also knew I couldn't mess with her. If I told her I'd deposit X amount on a particular day, I had to deliver; and I always did.

My mentors are also people who have seats on my bus. In fact, I believe mentors have some of the most important seats on

Chapter 3: Have the Right People on the Bus

any bus. In Ireland, grants are available for mentoring, which makes it much more accessible, even when you're just starting out. I've had many mentors over the years and have a couple on my bus even now. A mentor can be instrumental because they have travelled the road a bit longer than you have and can, therefore, give you advice that no one else can. It's absolute gold when you click with a mentor, so I urge you to take the time to find someone who can take that seat on your bus. As I do, you may end up with more than one mentor – the more people you can learn from, the better.

One of my most valued mentors is Sanjay, and he's certainly helped me in many ways over the years that I've known him. I vividly remember one particular conversation with him that completely flipped my perspective. I was driving from my house to Dungarvan in the early stages of the Covid-19 pandemic. It was incredibly stressful as we were managing our team, and client expectations, remotely. We had seven apartment blocks that we managed and I remember telling Sanjay that I hated managing them, and didn't want myself or my team to be spending time on them. I was convinced that if we got rid of them we'd have much more energy and capacity to do brilliant work.

Sanjay's reply turned on a light bulb in my head: "But Regina, you're running your own business. It's up to you to decide what type of business you want and what clients you have." It sounds so simple, but that was when I realised I did have the power to get rid of these apartment blocks. The income had always felt so huge that I didn't feel able to resign from them, but the more I talked to Sanjay, the more I could see he was right – I needed to get rid of those blocks.

Within a couple of days, I'd resigned our business as the managers for those seven blocks and, sure enough, we suddenly had much more capacity to do the work we really love and the business became more successful. When I analysed it, looking at the time and energy our team put into managing those blocks, it turned out to be a massive loss leader. If Sanjay hadn't been on my bus, I might never have had that realisation or wasted a few more years doing something that was just a thorn in my side.

Chapter 3: Have the Right People on the Bus

Finding clarity

During the Covid-19 pandemic, I felt very fuzzy about the direction my business was going in. I was struggling to find clarity on my own. This was when I came across John Paul, who coaches on leadership and management. He mentored me for six months and during that time I gained so much clarity on the foundations of the business that it's allowed us to grow to new levels.

He not only gave me clarity, but also a host of systems and processes to implement, which is what we have done over the past three years. Sometimes as a business owner you're doing so much in so many different places that it's difficult to achieve that level of clarity on your own.

Systems and processes are vital to building a strong and successful business though – these are like the engine of your bus, without them everything just stops running and you end up stuck at the side of the road. I'll talk more about implementing systems and processes in Chapter 7.

Within the business, our contractors are also very important people to have on the bus, whether they're plumbers, electricians or cleaners. We build strong relationships with our contractors by paying them on time, being loyal to them and being respectful. That said, they all know that if there is an issue with their work, we won't shy away from bringing it to their attention and having those big chats. If we need to have multiple chats with a particular contractor then they'll be asked to leave the bus!

But, the people on your bus don't just have to be those who have some interest or involvement in your business. Warren Buffett always says that it's important to consider who's in your inner circle, and that inner circle can just as easily be friends and family as a mentor or business partner. You want people on your bus who are going to help you thrive and support you in every area of your life, not just in your business.

For example, I have a few great friends who help me – Sheila, Grace, Aisling and Niall who have been on my bus over the years. Aisling and I solve the problems of the world at the crack of dawn when we walk the Cunnigar beach near home.

Chapter 3: Have the Right People on the Bus

Niall seems to have the answer to everything and is a real rock of a friend. Sheila owns a marketing agency called Márla Communications and we often talk about what works and what doesn't in our businesses. Grace works in finance and she is a smart cookie, and I've often bounced things off her. My cousin Denise has a big shot job in Aviation and she is super smart and practical and acts as a great sounding board for me. But, you might just invite a friend whose advice you value onto your bus – they don't have to be a business owner themselves to be able to provide support.

You may also find people who you want on your bus by networking. I recently participated in an event for International Women's Day with three amazing ladies, one of whom also works in property and has a great deal more experience in marketing property than I do. I spoke to her after the event and got some great nuggets of advice. The four of us who participated also agreed to meet up, as women in business, four times a year to share advice and help each other. These are the kinds of people I want on my bus – some of them know more than me and can help me grow, but others are at an earlier stage of their journey and I can share my knowledge and experience with them, helping them to grow.

LETTING PEOPLE ON AND OFF YOUR BUS

As I said earlier, not everyone will stay on your bus for the whole journey, but how you let people off your bus is really important. The ideal is to support people as they leave, rather than dropping them in the middle of nowhere with no idea about how to move forwards.

For example, there is one woman who's worked with me for 15 years, but more recently I could tell she wasn't as happy in her role as she had been. I approached her and simply said, "If you ever decide to leave, will you tell me way in advance so I can support and help you?" She agreed. Not long after that conversation, she gave us her notice, but she gave us eight weeks' notice!

I told her that if she wanted to stay for ten weeks, or even longer, if she hadn't found a job by the end of her notice period that she'd be welcome to. I made sure she got time off to go for interviews and I offered her coaching ahead of any job interviews if she'd like it. When she got off the bus, we were sad to see her go, but also happy for which bus and which journey she'd go on next.

Chapter 3: Have the Right People on the Bus

If someone wants to leave, you can't stop them. All you can do is create the best possible environment for them to thrive in. Even if you really want them to stay, you can't force them. You have to let them go and do so in the right way so that there is no bad feeling on either side. I've had people leave my team to set up a competing business, but there's no bad blood between us. I wished them well.

Sometimes, of course, you have to ask someone to get off the bus. In many situations, in my experience, when people are making a lot of mistakes at work it places a huge burden on their colleagues, as well as on the business. We all make mistakes from time to time, but when someone is making a lot of mistakes, not focusing and not learning, they impact absolutely everybody else. The poor performance of one individual can have a really damaging ripple effect across the entire business. I have seen it first hand where there is widespread loss of motivation and productivity. Other employees may become resentful and disengaged which ultimately leads to staff turnover. When people don't work out now, we try to make decisions quickly rather than drag it out.

I still find making these tough decisions hard, but if I've learned anything over the years, it's that this can't be put off. Often if someone isn't working out in the business, they aren't happy either. Not everyone is suited to the pace at which we work or the demands that come with it. In my company we want people who will own their mistakes when they happen – these are people who exhibit above the line behaviours of Ownership, Accountability and Responsibility (OAR), rather than below the line behaviours or Blame, Excuse, Deny (BED).

So, are the people in your company in the OAR camp or the BED camp? What I've found is that when you have clear values and a clear mission statement, it makes it much easier to have conversations about mistakes because it isn't personal – you can tie people's behaviour back to your company's values and maintain your standards. For example, we take pride in everything we do, so I might ask someone on the team, "Can you honestly tell me this is a piece of work you're proud of?"

We're also straight talking, so we don't beat around the bush with these conversations, or in our conversations with clients. We are happy to be direct and tell a client when an action they're proposing doesn't align with our values. At the same time, we're empathetic, so we'll listen and seek to understand when someone turns up in our office crying and upset because they can't get a rental home. People who encompass all of

Chapter 3: Have the Right People on the Bus

these qualities are the ones I want to bring onto my bus. You have to be clear about your own values and then you'll also start to see who you want on your bus.

In fact, how you get people on your bus is just as important as how you let them off. One of the biggest mistakes I've made is hiring in haste because we were under pressure – I can tell you now that it never works out. I'll also share that I only had this revelation about six months before I wrote this book – and I've been in business for 26 years! Hiring based on your values is essential, so you have to be careful who you let on your bus and when you let them take their seat. What you want to avoid is screeching to a halt at the side of the road to pick up a hitchhiker who looks like they will fit in, only to discover they don't get on with anyone else on your bus. You need to arrange to pick people up at the right point in your journey, and only let them on your bus when you're sure they'll work well with everyone else.

This is what we did with John, our general manager, who joined the business just months before I wrote this book. Maria and I knew we needed a manager at Liberty Blue – someone who could do all the audits and checks that neither Maria or myself had the time to do, and that we aren't particularly good at either. We also needed someone who could hold regular one-to-ones with our team and pick up the jobs that often got squeezed out of our calendars.

We didn't find John through traditional means. In fact, I met him when he hired me to sell a site. I could tell that even though John didn't have all the specific estate agency experience, he would be a great fit for the team. So, we spent a year "courting" him, he did some dry runs with us and when we were all confident it was the right fit he came on board.

When you're recruiting, always come back to your brand values, your mission and your vision. Does the person in front of you align with those? In our business, that means finding people who live up to our tagline of "Smarter, Faster, Better". If someone on our team takes ten hours to reply to a client email, that doesn't align with our values. If we put up with behaviour that doesn't align with ours, then everyone on the team suffers and so do our clients.

Of course, everyone makes mistakes and we shouldn't throw people under the bus when that happens. Instead we have to train them to help ensure they don't make the same mistake twice. When you can provide that clarity as the leader, and are willing to act as a coach, the right people for your bus will thrive.

Chapter 3: Have the Right People on the Bus

It is also beneficial to teach different members of your team how to do elements of other people's jobs, so that you don't end up panicking and hiring quickly when someone leaves unexpectedly, or is just off sick for more than a few days.

Sometimes people will get off your bus at one stop, only to rejoin you on your journey further down the road – but this will only happen if you allow them to leave in the right way. Cormac worked with us for ten years, but decided to leave as he wanted to take another direction. I kept in touch with him via social media, and I noticed that he was getting really good at social media marketing and promotion. So, two years after he left the business I asked if he'd come back, not to his old job, but to work in a social media marketing role. That was five years ago and it's been a fantastic journey for both of us as we've learned more about that space and defined what good looks like for the business together.

When someone you know comes back in a different capacity, it's easy to find them a seat on the bus because you already know they're the right fit for the team. For example, we needed to recruit someone part-time in recent weeks to cover while two of our team start estate agency college in September to become licensed estate agents. We designed an advert

81

designed for a part-time position and posted it across our social media channels. I got a message one evening over dinner from a lovely woman I knew through my son's former primary school. Anne Maria joined us a month ago and has fitted in brilliantly. She has a real can-do attitude and is fantastic with people. It was Sanjay, Gemma and Matt Giggs who really wised me up to how we should be looking for people for our business throughout our day-to-day interactions.

It's also important to mention that we are always striving to eliminate, automate or reduce activities. This comes from our mentor Tony. In addition, one of our brand values is that we love to innovate and our mission is to bring happiness to our customers, colleagues and community. By having this clarity and empowering our team it means they work on improving how we do things. As the business owner or manager, we don't want or need to be doing everything. A culture of innovation and improvement is important – in Liberty Blue it's expected. It also motivates and empowers our people. They get to implement the improvements, rather than just showing up for work. They are deal makers, not order takers. Ultimately all of this means they are exactly the kind of people we want on our bus.

Chapter 3: Have the Right People on the Bus

5 RULES FOR FINDING THE RIGHT PEOPLE TO GET ON YOUR BUS

#1 Always be looking for talent

One of the keys to finding the right people to join your team is to always be looking for talent, because then when you do need to replace someone quickly you will be much more likely to have someone who's the right fit lined up. My mentors Sanjay and Matt Giggs have been instrumental in helping me understand the need to constantly be looking for new people for my team, even when we don't have a vacant role.

If you start looking at who's already on your bus, you'll probably notice that they all have common traits. When I look at the people on my bus, whether they're employees, mentors or members of my inner circle, I see people who are helpful and people who are successful in their own right. Success leaves a trail, so when I'm looking for someone to coach or mentor me in particular, this is a key thing I look for.

However, I also want to stress that no-one is right all of the time. Sometimes what a coach or mentor suggests simply won't fit for your business and that's OK too – take what works for you and leave what doesn't.

#2 Begin with the end in mind

One of the best ways I've found to help me hire the right coaches over the years is to use the principle of "Begin with the end in mind" from Stephen R. Covey's book *The 7 Habits of Highly Effective People*.[4] I always set out very clearly what I want to achieve with their support by the end of a certain period.

You can take the same approach to setting goals for your business. Think about what you want to achieve in three and five years. Then reverse-engineer that so you can map out what and who you need to get you there. This will help you work out who should be getting on your bus and when you might need them. You also have to regularly evaluate the people you already have on your bus – are they the right ones to help you achieve your goals? Be honest if they aren't, because keeping them on your bus will only slow your progress towards your destination and, in the worst case, could derail it completely.

As the business owner, and therefore bus driver, there will be times when you need to let someone else take the wheel so you can have a break. When this happens, you need someone

---

4   Covey, S.R. (1997) *The Seven Habits of Highly Effective People: Restoring the Character Ethic.* Macmillan Reference USA.

Chapter 3: Have the Right People on the Bus

you trust, or a team you trust, who can step up and continue moving the bus forwards until you're in a position to get back in the driver's seat.

#3 Stick to your standards

Any weak links, whether they're employed staff or contractors, could have a negative effect on your business and the journey you're on. In our business, an unreliable contractor reflects badly on all of us. All it takes is for one person to not do what they say they will, when they say they will, and our whole brand could be tarnished. It's why it's so important to set standards and rigorously stick to them. You have to make sure that whoever is getting on your bus is prepared to maintain your standards as a bare minimum, and ideally exceed them whenever possible.

#4 Find people who challenge you

You are also looking for people who challenge you, because this can help you find new directions you would never have considered otherwise. Our marketing consultant Paula is particularly good at this and she challenges me all the time in a way that makes me think differently, and spot new opportunities.

#5 Don't forget about diversity

Diversity on your team is also really important and it's something we were missing for many years. Often when you hear about a lack of gender balance in the workplace, it's referring to having more men than women. At Liberty Blue, we flipped that on its head and for many years had far more women in the business than men. That has changed in the last year as we've brought more guys into the office. I've noticed that as a team we have more fun and there's more balance since we ensured there was a more even split between men and women on the team. They say men are from Mars and women are from Venus. We are wired differently and I've seen a lot of improvements in the business as a result of having a more gender-balanced team. The collaborative effort of everyone on the team has created richer diversity and an improvement to our bottom line. I think now looking back, having men on the team gives a better reflection to our customers. I believe we have a much wider perspective within the team and that is brilliant. Simply put, women benefit from working with men, and men benefit from working with women.

Chapter 3: Have the Right People on the Bus

THE NEED FOR RESILIENCE

There have been many times in my years in business when I've looked around and been really happy and excited about all the people on my bus. These are the times when everything is humming and you've hit the sweet spot, when *BANG* you hit a bump in the road, get a flat tyre and have to reset. That's just the nature of business.

As I write this, we've had one of these "bangs", but we've now got a new person on the bus. This little *BANG* has in fact helped us re-evaluate how we do things, and everyone is stepping up and working brilliantly as a team.

As the leader of any business, one of the most important qualities to possess is resilience. I'll come back to how to develop personal resilience in Chapter 11, but in short resilience is about being ready to deal with whatever happens. That doesn't mean you have to do everything alone though. Our mentor Tony, who was previously a CEO in a massive US company, has helped us with the recruitment process by conducting interviews and preparing the job description for our new hires, alongside our manager John. I had a few tough days at one stage and was able to vent to Tony (or as I sometimes call him, my business therapist).

We need other people to help us get through these difficult times, but we also need others to enable us to achieve success – we can't go on this journey alone. We need the right people on our bus not only for the resources they bring, but also for their wisdom and to help us learn. When you have mentors and coaches who have seen the road ahead, learning from them can help you fast-forward your success by avoiding mistakes they may have made and by seeing situations from a different perspective.

We also need those on our team to be resilient and that also means they are able to take feedback really well. We are straight talking and it creates a difficult environment if we have to beat around the bush because we're afraid of making some-one cry when we provide constructive feedback. I recently had a situation where one of my team didn't get a sign placed at a new homes development and instead left it for someone else to do, without checking that it had been done. When I talked to him about this, and stressed the need to check everything because what doesn't get checked doesn't get done, he took

Chapter 3: Have the Right People on the Bus

the feedback incredibly well and thanked me for it. This guy will go far in life.

You need resilient people on your bus, those who are OAR characters (they own it, they are accountable and they take responsibility). Having that type of person on the team makes for a happy environment, which is absolutely essential in my view.

Good people help us live our vision, whether they're colleagues, coaches, business stakeholders, family or friends. These are the people we need in the seats on our bus and we have to be prepared to let those who don't support our vision get off, rather than taking them along for the ride and slowing everyone down in the process.

Steps for success

- Know your destination – work on the business as well as in it so you can lead your team.

- Build strong relationships – not everyone on your bus has to be a member of staff.

- Let people go – when someone isn't the right fit, help them to leave sooner rather than later.

- Always be hiring – look out for right-fit people, whether you have a vacancy to fill or not.

- Work on having a rock star training culture – people thrive when they are learning and growing.

- Check and audit your processes and systems – things may not always be as they seem. This is *very* important.

CHAPTER 4

DO THE RIGHT THING

Doing the right thing is closely connected to doing things right the first time. Although they sound very similar, they are subtly different. They are foundational for our business and, I believe, are among the reasons why we've been successful. But I'd like to be clear from the start – first time right does not mean everything has to be perfect. I have high standards, but I wouldn't describe myself as a perfectionist. It might sound like a subtle distinction, but it's an important one.

The definition of perfection is, "The action or process of improving something until it is faultless." Will anything in your business ever be truly faultless? I would say probably not. Doing things right the first time is about committing to a journey of continuous improvement, rather than striving for perfection which you'll never reach.

When it comes to getting things right the first time, there are two main principles to bear in mind: the devil is in the detail and begin with the end in mind.

THE DEVIL IS IN THE DETAIL

In the world of residential property, one of the most important aspects of selling someone's home is the photos you take of the property. We know that this is what attracts buyers and that poor quality photos will put people off, even if the property itself has a lot going for it. Knowing this, it baffles me when I see photos of homes on property websites with grocery bags and other items cluttering a kitchen surface, or bedrooms with unmade beds. We know that great photos sell homes, so why would we ignore these important details when we know they make all the difference?

Noticing those details is the first step. Making sure you address them, whether that's by putting the groceries in a cupboard,

Chapter 4: Do the Right Thing

making a bed or even moving a rubbish bin out of sight is the second, and it's this second step that allows you to do it right the first time.

Focusing on the details has always been how I've approached my life and work – remember my story about the film director and the firelighters from the first chapter? That is a moment that still sticks with me and reminds me why the small details are important. Another such moment came in around 2000, when I was running my first business Blue Chip Marketing and Events, but I had learned from my experience with Jim Sheridan the film maker.

Waterford Crystal were hosting a big conference and we beat off stiff competition to win the contract to run it for them. This wasn't just a big deal for the reputation of the business, we needed the income from this event to be able to keep operating. On the day of the conference, everything was ready and the stage was set up with a podium for the speakers to stand at. However, one of the speakers was an MEP who was a wheelchair user – I didn't want the podium to be in his way when he went on stage, so I arranged for it to be moved to the side for his slot.

Immediately after this MEP's speaking slot, the CEO of Waterford Crystal would be stepping on stage to speak. I didn't want him to be without the podium, so I also arranged for it to be moved back into place as soon as the MEP left the stage. Some people might have felt like this was all a bit over the top and that I was worrying about nothing. But the first thing the CEO of Waterford Crystal said when he stepped up to speak was, "Well done to the organisers, I was worried about that podium." People notice the details – and they notice and appreciate it when you take care of them without them having to ask.

BEGIN WITH THE END IN MIND

I mentioned this concept in the last chapter in relation to finding the right people for your business, and it also holds true here. It really helps to walk in the shoes of your customer and to view your business from their perspective. What do they see when they walk into your office? What will their experience as a buyer or seller be like, from start to finish? Once you understand what your customers see, you are better placed to make changes that will improve their experience. But how do you know what you should improve? The answer is by thinking

Chapter 4: Do the Right Thing

about the outcome you want. When you know how you want your customers to feel at the end of their interactions with you, it makes it easier to identify which parts of your process may need to change or be refined.

When you begin with the end in mind, you focus on the details and this will also lead you to the right thing to do. Let's imagine you're preparing for an event, ask yourself what you want the people who attend to say when they leave. What do you want them to talk about? What will they remember? For example, you want them to enjoy the food so you have to make sure you hire good caterers, but the food isn't the only important detail – how are they going to eat it? Will they need plates and cutlery and somewhere to sit down, or are you serving snacks they can eat with their hands? Do you need serviettes? If you're serving drinks what kinds of cups or glasses will you provide? Who is going to serve the food and drinks? Who is going to clear up throughout the event? It's these small details that can make or break an experience. They are the difference between doing the right thing and making people feel wonderful, and not doing enough which leaves people apathetic, or even worse means they have a bad experience.

YOU WON'T ALWAYS BE RIGHT FIRST TIME AND YOU WON'T BE PERFECT

Although we strive to get things right the first time, we don't always manage it. Sometimes we make a mistake; sometimes something outside of our control goes wrong. This is where doing the right thing becomes very important because, in those circumstances, the right thing to do is apologise and own the mistake. We're all human and we all make mistakes from time to time. The mistake often isn't what a client will remember though, it's how we handle that mistake that will stick in their mind.

If you apologise, own the mistake and take steps to ensure it doesn't happen again, a client will remember that and you will be doing the right thing. I like to uncover the root cause of a problem, so I examine not only what happened, but why it happened. Was it down to a lack of training? Do we have the wrong person on the bus? Was it a miscommunication? When you understand the why, you can fix the how.

It's also important to accept that you won't achieve "perfect", and you have to be careful that in striving for perfection you don't overwork or burn yourself out. I know that, personally,

Chapter 4: Do the Right Thing

the biggest loser when I'm striving for perfection is my own energy. I will push myself to do whatever it takes to get something over the line and to make it as good as it can be. However, I will admit that working long hours and not taking care of myself hasn't always stood me in good stead in terms of my health. I'm getting better at knowing when to ease off for my own good, which is something I'll talk about in more detail in Chapter 11, but driving yourself into the ground in pursuit of perfection is not the right thing to do, for you or your business.

YOU CAN'T LEAVE THIS TO CHANCE

Doing the right thing, and doing it right the first time, can't be left to chance – it's a process-driven exercise. You have to work through every step on your customer's journey with you and create a process or system for every one of them. How should everyone in your office answer the phone? What process should your agents follow during a valuation? For instance, in our business, if we're doing a valuation and having a conversation about selling a property we make sure we have that conversation with the homeowner in their favourite room. The conversation isn't just about valuing the property, it's an opportunity for us to understand the seller's needs.

It's no different with a buyer – we seek to understand their pain points and what they want to achieve. We're applying the principle of "begin with the end in mind" to our clients as well, because when we know their end goal, we can work backwards to uncover all the steps we need to take to help them achieve it. Maria and I have spent years honing our processes, we share stories and constantly check in with one another about how different things worked. We didn't write the book on this – we have studied with some of the best estate agency coaches in the business. We are on a journey of continuous learning and improvement.

Communication is one of the most important factors for delivering a positive customer experience. Silence is the enemy – I always think of silence and poor communication like the flatline on a heart rate monitor in a hospital. To me, a lack of communication means you're not there, you're dead, so we make a point of keeping all of our clients, whether buyers or sellers, in the loop with what's happening. If we're selling property for someone who doesn't live locally, we'll tell them when a viewing is booked in, for instance. It's these small touch points that show you care and that you have the client in mind.

Chapter 4: Do the Right Thing

COME BACK TO YOUR VALUES AND MISSION

Having clarity over your values, mission and vision will help everyone in your business to do the right thing. These provide a very clear guide that everyone can follow – they are like a compass that helps steer everyone in the same, and the right, direction.

As an example, John had found a buyer, a young woman, for an apartment in the city where there is an issue with drugs. He called me and asked whether he should tell her about the issues in this part of town. "She's a young woman Regina, and it's not really sitting right with me, what should I do? Should I tell her about the issues in the area?"

I agreed that was the right thing to do, so he called her, even though the sale was agreed, and said, "Hi Hazel, it's John from Liberty Blue here. Look, I've been thinking about this and while the apartment itself is gorgeous and the building is being kept much better since the new management company took it over (we never managed this building by the way), I'd just like to tell you that there are some drug issues in the area right now. I was just worried that you might not be aware that it might be dangerous for you."

Hazel replied, "Thank you. My uncle actually warned me about this and I've lived in rougher places, so I still want to go ahead, but I really appreciate the call."

In this example, we were always going to sell the property for our client, whether it was bought by Hazel or not, but to do the right thing we have to match the right people to the right property. As it turned out Hazel bought the apartment, but if she had decided to back out after John's call we would have found someone else better suited to that location.

Within the estate agency business in particular, another area where it's important we stay true to our values and make sure we do the right thing is in giving honest valuations. Some agents might overvalue a property because they think that's what the seller wants to hear. Our approach is to always give honest valuations and to explain that these are based on market evidence. What we want to avoid is over-promising and under-delivering, and we do that by being realistic and fair with our valuations. Then, with great marketing and service, we hope to exceed the client's expectations.

Chapter 4: Do the Right Thing

There are certain situations when doing the right thing is obvious, with no grey areas, because there is one course of action that is morally right and one that isn't. We've had the odd landlord ask us to do things that weren't legal in the past – that's clearly a straightforward "no", because you can't do something illegal, even if it's what your client wants

Doing the right thing isn't only about doing what's right for your clients though, it's also about doing what's right for you and your team. Not so long ago, a gentleman who was giving us some new business called me on my mobile at 10pm. I answered because I assumed it was urgent, but it quickly became obvious that he just wanted to discuss renting his property out. I told him I'd been asleep and had only answered as I'd assumed it was urgent, but that I would call him in the morning to discuss this. He apologised and sounded a bit embarrassed – he works in the medical field and said that this was the first chance he had to call me.

Years ago, I would probably have handled that call very differently, but I've learned the importance of setting clear boundaries for myself and my team, and of setting these out with clients from the beginning of our relationship. In my opinion, the only time it's acceptable to take a call about a new piece of business at 10pm is when it's pre-arranged and it's at that time because there's a major difference in time zone! In this instance, the gentleman didn't pick up when I called him the next morning, but he did call me back at lunchtime and I was able to talk him through our services, including the out-of-hours line we have for emergencies.

I've learned from previous experience, and from handling a client relationship poorly from the beginning. One of the most high maintenance clients we ever had used to call me at 7.30pm and I would take his calls. In doing so, I blurred the boundaries and he respected me less for it.

Mutual respect is the foundation for any successful relationship, whether that's business or pleasure. Our mission is to create great experiences that make our customers happy. It's about having a deeper understanding of every detail from start to finish and, along the way, it's about keeping our team involved, engaged and inspired.

We want to *bring happiness to our customers, colleagues and community, and to be helpful experts and champions of Waterford, showcasing that it is a great place to live.* We deliver happiness for our customers through our straight-talking advice and going

Chapter 4: Do the Right Thing

the extra mile. We're helpful experts for our customers and our community, which is where our "Live After 5s" on social media come in, as well as our monthly webinars.

Doing the right thing is one of the values that helps us achieve this mission, so is having pride in everything we do. Our office looks beautiful, inside and out. It's always clean and tidy, which is the right thing to do so it's essential for our business. We take beautiful photos, because this brings happiness to our customers – it's the right thing to do and it ties back into our overarching mission as a business.

Sometimes we have to remind the people on our team that we take pride in what we do – you can imagine Maria's reaction when one of the team took a photo of a house for sale with two bins in front of it! The great thing about being clear about our values is that when you have to have a difficult conversation or correct someone, you can bring it back to the values, brand personality and mission. It's not personal and we need to be consistent – needless to say there have been no more photos with bins in them since because we take pride in what we do.

Because we have such a clear idea of who we are and what we do, we are able to deliver consistently on our mission. But consistency comes from having a process around what we do.

For example, our process for being helpful experts is to run a "Live After 5" every Monday to Friday, and at least three to four out of these five is just a helpful tip, we're not selling anything. Similarly, our monthly webinars aren't an opportunity for us to sell, they are an opportunity to provide helpful, expert advice to our community, either from members of our team or other experts who we bring into speak.

This does take a lot of effort, but it has really helped us grow our social media audiences and trust levels within our community. It definitely has helped us grow the business and win more listings – it works and helps us stand out because nobody else in Ireland is doing this. It's also worth noting the importance of YouTube. We add all of our videos to our YouTube channel because it's a great resource, like a library, with loads of content and it's brilliant for search engine optimisation (SEO). If you want to see what I mean, check out Terry Gorry, the Irish solicitor, on YouTube – he has a huge following and some brilliant content.

Chapter 4: Do the Right Thing

Everyone on our team lives and breathes our values and mission. This doesn't happen by accident, this is part of their induction and it's baked into our company culture. We have our mission and values on our office wall and we talk about them in team meetings. We even screen job candidates to make sure their values align with ours – if someone doesn't pass the values interview it doesn't matter how good their credentials are, they won't be getting on our bus. The times we have deviated from this course of action, it has not worked out well for us.

STRIVE FOR CONTINUOUS IMPROVEMENT

As I said earlier, we won't always get things right, but we acknowledge when we have made a mistake or when there is an area in which we could improve. The onboarding of new staff members was an area that needed a lot of improvement, and it's one we've been working on in the past couple of years. Someone in one of my mastermind groups recommended Trainual, which is employee onboarding software, and we started using it. It's provided more structure to our onboarding.

We approached this process in the same way we approach the customer journey – we started with the end in mind by thinking about how a new employee will feel on their first day and what they need to know. With this in mind, it was much easier to design the onboarding, but this is still a work in progress. We are refining it and improving it as we go, based on feedback from the people who have been through that process at the business, because it's such an important part of the employee experience and it's part of how we can deliver happiness to our colleagues.

HOW TO MAKE SURE YOU'RE DOING THE RIGHT THING IN YOUR BUSINESS

To ensure everyone in your business is doing the right thing, and doing things right the first time, you have to make sure you have the right foundations in place. This comes back to what I talked about in Chapters 2 and 3.

Start by being very clear about where you are going and what you want to achieve. *Begin with the end in mind.* You have to step out of the doing to give yourself space to plan and strategise. Ask yourself what *you* want in the next three, five and ten years.

Chapter 4: Do the Right Thing

Set out a long-term strategy for your business. Once you know what your strategy is, you can work out all the processes and steps you need to take to get to that goal. Your strategy may well include several aspects, but as you work through this exercise you'll realise they all support one another.

At Liberty Blue, one of our long-term goals is to win more sales listings and rental listings but there are various things we have to do to win that business. Part of this strategy for us is to position ourselves as helpful experts; and to grow our profile as the expert voice in the property industry in our area. We can do this by making time for marketing meetings and working closely with our marketing consultant to create a plan of action and, here's the key, follow that up with meticulous execution.

You can have all the dreams and plans in the world, but unless you follow those up with action, nothing is going to happen. Along the way, you need to set tangible metrics to aim for, otherwise you won't know when you've succeeded. For example, we wanted to get more Google reviews for the business, so we set ourselves a target of having 500 Google reviews by Christmas 2022. In the end, it took us until January to hit that number, but we got there and we haven't stopped. Now we have a new target of 750 Google reviews by Christmas 2023. As I write this in October we have 702 google reviews.

There are many reasons that we're focusing on Google reviews, but the underlying one is that it brings the trust factor to the business. When you have this trust factor, it improves your ranking in search engine results pages – in other words it's part of our SEO strategy. But we can't get all of these reviews without having a process and system for collecting them. We've found the right way to reach out to clients for a review and we make sure that we do so consistently. How do you get more Google reviews? Ask! Ask, and ask again. People are busy, so you might have to remind them a few times. We find texting and emailing the request works very well. Also, it's important that collecting reviews is part of the team's targets. After all, what gets measured gets done. That works for us.

We haven't always got this right the first time, but we have tested things, refined them and then gone again. I said at the start of this chapter that the aim is not perfection, it's striving for continuous improvement. This is particularly important when you are trying new things, because if you wait for them to be perfect you won't do anything.

Chapter 4: Do the Right Thing

If you're finding that the desire for everything to be perfect is holding you back from taking any action, my advice is to start small. Roll out a new process to a small number of clients, get feedback, make improvements and go again, gradually increasing the number of people each time.

Creating your plan and executing it isn't where this ends though – you have to regularly review the plan to make sure it is still delivering what you need and helping you work towards your business' mission. Share the results you're seeing with your team to keep them motivated and to reinforce that you are all doing the right things to achieve your goals. If you introduce something new, make sure you provide appropriate training to your team so that they know what good looks like, are clear on what the right thing to do is in any given situation, and know how to do it right the first time.

Training is the bedrock of having a successful team. This isn't just a journey of continuous improvement for you as the business owner, it's also a journey of continuous improvement for your team and you want every person who's on your bus to be committed to growing personally and professionally.

Steps for success

- Get clear on your mission and values – use them to help you create your roadmap.

- Share your mission, values and roadmap with your team – make sure everyone is on the same page.

- Be specific – set time frames and measurable metrics for your goals.

- Be consistent – commit to your actions and follow through on all of them.

- Make sure you have the right people on the bus! This is EVERYTHING!

CHAPTER 5

BE A CHALLENGER

What does being a challenger really mean? For me, it's all about standing out and not blending in. It's about challenging the status quo and finding better ways of working. There is a lot more talk these days about challenger brands, but being a challenger isn't restricted to business, it's a mentality and it's one I've had my entire life…

IN THE BLUE CORNER...

One of my favourite films has always been *Rocky*.[5] You can't beat the music, and I love that iconic scene of Sylvester Stallone running up the steps outside the Philadelphia Museum of Art. I'd listen to the *Rocky* theme when I was training at the gym because I found it so inspiring – when I heard the horns at the start of that song, I'd feel as though I could do anything. Then I got this notion, *Jesus wouldn't I love to be in a boxing fight...*

The universe took note. In 2015, someone approached me and asked if I'd consider entering a white collar boxing fight for charity. Before I could think too long about it, I said yes. They say the definition of luck is opportunity meeting preparation – I had the opportunity, now it was time to fully prepare. When I first agreed to the boxing match, I was training at the gym about three times a week and was in pretty good shape, but I knew I needed to do more.

I fully committed and told people I was going to be part of this white collar boxing event for the Heart Foundation – there was

---

5   *Rocky (1976) - IMDb* (1976). Available at: https://www.imdb.com/title/tt0075148/.

Chapter 5: Be a Challenger

no getting out of it – and I worked with my trainer to increase and change my training regime. I also had to change my diet for three months in the lead up to getting into the ring – I also had to give up red wine, which I enjoy very much at weekends. Both the training and my diet were quite extreme for those three months, but it worked. I especially loved the training, which was really gritty, and by fight night I was lean and super fit.

Even though I was very well prepared, I felt extremely nervous about the fight in the two weeks beforehand. I knew I needed to get my mind in the right place on the day, so I stayed at the hotel that was hosting the fight the night before getting in the ring and it was then that I felt much calmer and was able to psych myself up in a positive way. The hype on the night was incredible. There were about 500 people in the room and I walked to the ring with a group of my friends accompanying me dressed up in Star Wars outfits – they looked amazing. But as I climbed into the ring I was suddenly alone and what I was about to do hit me – I nearly vomited. *Oh sweet, divine Jesus, what have I signed up for?!*

I pushed those thoughts out of my mind and focused on my opponent, who was a good 15 years younger than me and super fit. As soon as the referee brought us together to tap gloves, my focus was on one thing and one thing only: winning that fight. And what a fight it was.

We traded blows over multiple rounds – she might have been younger than I was, but I knew I'd out-trained her. At one point I could see she was tiring and… I paused… It took me about two years to let that one go! I should have just kept going and then I would probably have won the fight, but as it was it went to the judges' decision and she won by a whisker. Our fight was named "Fight of the Night" though and even though I didn't win, I still felt a huge sense of achievement and satisfaction for having done it.

As I left that hotel with my black eye, exhausted but exhilarated, I thought about what I'd loved most about the experience – the challenge. It wasn't just the challenge of stepping into the ring, but also the challenge of the training and strict diet. The feeling I got from that was just off the Richter scale.

I did what I set out to do and achieved my dream of fighting in a boxing match. Crazy when I look back, but I did it. I was so proud to see my seven-year-old son in the crowd with his banner cheering me on. Sometimes in business it's only when we look back that we recognise what we have achieved.

Chapter 5: Be a Challenger

BECOMING A BUSINESS CHALLENGER

There are a lot of parallels between fitness and business – for a start you won't be an overnight success in either of them. It takes discipline and work to succeed, whether you're working towards lifting heavier weights at the gym or building a thriving business. You have to show up and put the time in. You need to commit to your business goals in the same way you commit to your fitness goals.

Once you commit to those goals, it's essential to block out the time to working *on* your business as opposed to only working *in* your business. When I signed up for that boxing match, I had to push through the pain and fear and it's no different when you're building a business. I can't tell you how many times I've gone into meetings scared or worried, but no matter how scared you are or how difficult a conversation might be, you need to just do it. You can't avoid those situations in business. This is about building the resilience that enables you to challenge. You need to be able to rise above and ignore your critics and the haters (which I'll talk more about in Chapter 10). We all want approval from our peers and to be liked by our staff, but if you know you're doing the right thing you have to be able to move forward even without that approval and challenge anyway.

If you are having problems with an employee who isn't performing or who has a bad attitude it's really important you deal with it. It's important you have a straight-talking conversation and this is where regular one-to-one meetings are very effective. These aren't always easy, but as I get older it gets easier to have those difficult conversations. Begin with the end in mind. Think about what good looks like. What improvement do you want from your employee? See it from their point of view and listen – maybe they need more support, training or clarity around your expectations – being a challenger doesn't mean you can't pause and listen to others.

That said, setting out your stall as to what you expect is really important. You provide the clarity, the environment, the training and then you measure, measure and measure some more. As I always say, what gets measured and checked gets done. You need to hold people accountable, but also as the owner or boss of the business you have to provide clarity, lead, motivate and help your team grow. Investing in our people is the smartest way to grow our businesses, in fact it's the only way in my opinion.

Chapter 5: Be a Challenger

THE BIRTH OF LIBERTY BLUE

In 1997, I set up my first business, Bookaroom, which special-
ised in property management. This was a challenger brand of
its own, as it was the first business of its kind in South-East
Ireland. But in 2015 we made a big decision – we were going
to move into the property sales sector and rebrand as Liberty
Blue. I made this decision with Maria, our director, and Paula,
our marketing consultant.

The property sales sector was crowded. We would have 53
direct competitors. It was time to ask ourselves some important questions: Did we want to fit in and blend in? Did we want
to look the same as everyone else? The answers came easily:
No! It was Paula who introduced us to the term "challenger
brand" and it immediately resonated with us. We were there
to challenge the status quo – we didn't want to blend in or do
what everyone else did. We wanted to set ourselves apart for
all the right reasons.

This started with our logo – Maria suggested a ladybird because she brings luck and abundance wherever she goes. We
wanted something earthy, and that's very unusual in our space.
We chose to use "Blue" in our name, because blue is the colour

of Waterford. We wanted a name we loved and were proud of, and a brand that could stand strong alongside others. When we were designing our new logo and choosing the name of the business, I wanted something that would look just as impressive as Savills if we were alongside them. If you're not sure how you feel about the name of your business when you're setting it up, just imagine how you'll feel when you're handing your business card or brochure out to people and that name is on the front.

Make way for the Incredible Hulk

I didn't necessarily realise it at the time, but Bookaroom was also a challenger brand. Like I said at the beginning of this chapter, being a challenger is a mentality – it's not restricted to your business. When we were running Bookaroom and wanted to run a promotion for student accommodation, we got a giant Incredible Hulk, branded it up with the Bookaroom logo and signs saying, "Looking for student accommodation? Call this number", and positioned it on the busiest roundabout in Waterford near the train station. This was before the days of social media, but it went viral. It was in the papers, people were talking about it on radio shows, and even travelling to

Chapter 5: Be a Challenger

take pictures of it! We loved the idea; it was bold and it got people talking about our business. After the roundabout, we moved the Hulk and put him next to a landmark building in Waterford and it was the same story. It was big, bold and it got us noticed.

How can you stand out? In today's world of social media, we have so many ideas. I would suggest you take inspiration from estate agents all over the world and find what works for you. Instagram and TikTok are great places to look – there are so many resources. Why not find your own mastermind group and see what is working for your peers? Ultimately though, it's about creating video content as I write this. If you aren't producing video, you're making a big mistake – don't be worrying about how you look and sound and don't wait for perfection. I promise you, the more you do, the better you will get.

SMALL DETAILS, BIG IMPACT

Our marketing is – and always has been – very customer-centric. We make sure we understand our customers and their pain points and challenges so that we can address those in a way that's aligned with who we are. Everything we do is for our customers. We also look for the small ways in which we can stand out. One example is that we don't display properties in the windows of our office. Initially we swapped the property photos for giant pictures of Maria and myself in the window. Maria cringed at this idea at first, but I pointed out that it would have the desired effect and get people talking about us – if they loved it, they'd talk about it; if they didn't like it, they'd talk about it; if it stood out, they'd talk about it. And they did, it was all part of our challenger brand. We first tried this a couple of years after we rebranded as Liberty Blue because we wanted to get people's attention and do something different to all the other estate agents in town. Now we don't even have those photos, we just have a clear window. I've noticed a few estate agents recently in our area take the same approach, wherever did they get that idea!

You might think that's an odd decision for an estate agency, but rarely has anyone *ever* come to us and said they were going to buy, sell or rent a property because they saw it in our window. When you think about it, that's not so surprising – the majority of people don't choose to buy or sell property by walking past an estate agents office. In my opinion and experience, it's more that it's become an expectation to see properties in the

Chapter 5: Be a Challenger

window of an estate agent rather than it serving a truly valuable purpose. Maybe that's not as true in a big city like London, but in Waterford that's not how people make those kinds of decisions. But throughout the estate agency business there's a perception that you need properties on display in your window.

Another reason we removed the properties from our window is that our ethos is all about being transparent and straight talking – we wanted people to be able to look inside, see us and see how we're working. Until much more recently, we had a wall of properties on display in our office, but we've removed that as well because we want our office to be an inviting space – a lot of the research shows that people find going to see estate agents intimidating. We've worked hard to make our office into a collaborative space and an environment people want to be in.

Lisa Novak really inspired me with her amazing offices in Australia, which don't look at all like an estate agency business, but more like a boutique hotel. I didn't get to recreate Lisa's office, but I took inspiration from it.

We're progressive with how we approach the interior design of our office too – we've decorated it in colours that aren't standard for an estate agency and we even engaged an interior designer to make sure the space was welcoming, represented us and our brand personality and that it stood out.

PUTTING YOURSELF OUT THERE

We also embraced video and started posting on social media very early in our journey as a brand – I still remember Daniel, from Nest Seekers (an international property brokerage firm featured on BBC now), telling me back in 2016 that we needed to build a presence on social media and, as he explained it, "build a tribe". He wasn't a mentor, but someone who has given me great advice over the years. It was him who suggested that I start doing videos and that I do "Lives". I wasn't aware of anyone in Ireland at the time who was producing video content (even now very few do) and I've never been one to let an opportunity pass me by so, on my way home, I did my very first Live at the airport. I didn't wait until I had everything "perfect", I didn't plan what I was going to say, I just turned on my video and started talking.

In the early days of producing videos, I pre-recorded most of them. I cringe when I look back now because those videos of me sharing tips are so formal, but it's been a journey and you

Chapter 5: Be a Challenger

have to start somewhere! These days we do Lives regularly (every day during the week in fact) and record videos much more on the fly. One of my top tips is to keep your videos relaxed and to not make them overly formal, especially when you're just sharing some advice. The exception is videos designed to showcase a property, in which case you want to produce them more formally so that they look really slick.

Our video strategy on social media is very aligned to our vision and mission – we're helpful experts who bring happiness to our community. This is where our Live After 5s come in, which are just me sharing advice. Whereas our videos showcasing a client's property always look incredibly professional and demonstrate our property expertise.

In business finding people that we admire who are successful is a great way of upping our game. For example some of the people I take inspiration from are Ian Storey in Cheshire and Sean Barrett. Both of these UK estate agents sell luxury homes and do beautiful marketing – I say beautiful because their photos are beautiful and their videos are fantastic.

If you want to create video content, my advice is to start with short videos and don't compare yourself to anyone else. Yes, use their content to inspire you, but remember you have to start somewhere. The best person to guide you on this, in my opinion, is Christopher Watkins. Chris helps estate agents grow their businesses and he has definitely inspired me a lot. You can follow him on Facebook and LinkedIn. He rightly advises that you tell a story rather than post a photo of a house marked "sold".

The key thing when it comes to video is getting started. There are so many ideas and resources online, such as YouTube, that you can easily find inspiration. A top tip when starting out is to find agent videos you like and use some of their themes to create your own content with your own style. It's very, very important that you are authentic. Giving helpful, expert advice without looking for anything in return is one of the most effective things you can do and a fantastic way to grow your audience online.

Earlier I mentioned Irish solicitor Terry Gorry who is on LinkedIn and has a YouTube following of over 24,000 subscribers. All of Terry's content is around giving his audience value and helpful tips and advice. I think he is a fantastic example of the effectiveness of video. The other thing to mention is that he is super consistent – consistency is essential to success. Be consistent

Chapter 5: Be a Challenger

with your content because your audience needs to know that you are consistently showing up with helpful information. I'm not going to lie, this does require a big effort and sometimes investment in resources, but it does pay off. Also, the more videos you do the better you get. Just like driving a car it's very difficult in the beginning (well, I certainly found it difficult when I started driving) and then you just drive without even thinking about what you have to do. After a while, appearing on video will be the same.

KEEP IT CONSISTENT

If you want to be a challenger brand, you have to be consistent with your actions and your messaging. A challenger doesn't challenge one day, disappear the next and then reappear six months later to challenge something else. If you're going to challenge, you have to challenge all the time – just like in boxing you have to keep up with a consistent training regime and diet if you want to have a chance of winning your fights.

In the world of being a challenger, it's all about being consistent – you can't worry about whether people like you or like everything you're doing. Not everyone is going to like you, that's just life. But equally, my business isn't just me – there's Maria, and now also Darragh, John, Murt, Anne Marie, Veresia, Lianna and Aaron, plus all of our contractors and advisers.. I've encouraged all of them to record videos and become faces for the business too. That's really unusual in Ireland, where mainly the sole face of most businesses is the owner.

How you challenge in your space will evolve as your business does. I look back on some of the things we've done in the past and I know we wouldn't necessarily do them now, but they were the right thing to do at the time.

EMBRACE THE CHALLENGER MENTALITY

One of the keys is to work with people who challenge you – Maria is one of those people for me. We've worked together for just coming up to 20 years now and she often challenges my ideas. Maria is the yin in the business and I am the yang. Over the years our different personalities and skills have complimented the business and each other hugely. This has been a major ingredient in our business success. Paula, our marketing consultant, is another person who challenges me and I love her for it. I remember one particularly heated marketing meeting

Chapter 5: Be a Challenger

we had in the early days of our relationship. I called her afterwards and said, "I never, ever want you to stop challenging me. I've thought about it and you're right, everything you said was right." She continues to challenge me and I know I need that because not every idea of mine will be a good one.

You can also encourage others to embrace the challenger mentality. When we were first starting out, we were taking on other business alongside property at times to help us in those early days. One such example was event organising. For two years, we'd organised a maritime festival because the business badly needed the income. As other business came in, we were able to focus more on the core business of property. Three weeks before the next festival, the organiser called me and said, "We need your help."

The long and short of it was that they only had about 50 people booked to attend the maritime ball that was arranged for 300 people – they wanted us to sell 250 tickets in three weeks. I didn't even know if we could do it and, because of the tight deadline, I charged three times what I had been for our services – and to be honest, we needed the extra income it would generate. My back was against the wall and I was going to need all of my resources to deliver.

The challenge was that, with the event black tie and only three weeks away, many of the people we spoke to either weren't available or didn't fancy hiring a tux on that short notice. I needed to get creative. All the money was going to charity, so I hit on the idea of offering the people who couldn't attend the chance to buy a bear for their seat instead. They could have their company name on the teddy bear and they'd still be supporting the charity – but they wouldn't have to worry about hiring a tux.

When I pitched it to the organiser his initial reaction was "That's a ridiculous idea!" But as I explained that none of the bears would eat dinner, and that he'd make pure profit from each one sold (as I could get the bears for free), he came around to the idea. In the end I sold those 250 tickets by offering people who couldn't attend the chance to purchase a bear instead, *and* we auctioned the bears off at the end of the night, raising about €7,000 extra for the charity! This is the essence of thinking differently and embracing the challenger mentality – it allows you to not only achieve your targets, but to smash them. We ended up with a packed ballroom and did incredibly well financially.

Chapter 5: Be a Challenger

Setting ambitious targets for yourself and your business is part of being a challenger. Even if other people don't realise what you're capable of yet, you need to have the confidence to put yourself out there and test your methods. Before we officially rebranded as Liberty Blue and announced to the world that we were moving into property sales, I told my hairdresser I would sell her house for her. She'd had it on the market with an agent for three months and hadn't had a single offer. "I'm just going to give it to three agents now and that's it," she told me.

"Look, give it to me and I'll have a sale agreed in four weeks," I replied. My hairdresser agreed and I walked away thinking *Oh Jesus, now I have to sell this house*. It felt like a huge challenge, but as soon as I visited the house I could see why it hadn't sold. It was very clear when I put myself in the shoes of a buyer — there were very bright colours, the beds weren't dressed, in one room there was a bunk bed that was eating up a lot of space. No wonder she hadn't had any offers. When you're selling property, what you're actually selling is space, so the key is staging. Moving furniture around, painting the house, dressing beds and making a better first impression is key to selling homes well.

To my hairdresser's credit, she was brilliant and did everything I asked of her to make the property more appealing. It worked – I had a sale agreed in seven days. I hadn't done what the other agent had, I'd approached things differently and I got a great result. It's hugely important for us as agents to go the extra mile and give our clients the right advice as to how to present their house well to prospective buyers. Mostly, buyers can't imagine themselves in rooms with purple walls or see their furniture in cluttered rooms. We'll get the beds dressed and the house painted if the client needs this service. I knew there and then that Liberty Blue would be able to challenge the established agencies.

HOW TO BECOME A CHALLENGER

As I've said, the defining characteristic of the challenger mentality is a desire to stand out, rather than blend in. Within a business setting, however, you can't just challenge for the sake of challenging – you need to challenge because you know doing things differently will get results. It's really important that your challenger mentality is guided by the values and mission of your business, because this will help you work out what direction to go in as a challenger brand.

Chapter 5: Be a Challenger

For example, part of our mission at Liberty Blue is to be helpful experts and this drives a lot of our decisions – it's why we have consistently shown up for our Live After 5s and why we are so active on social media. It's also why we host our monthly webinars and, because we include all of this insightful, helpful content in our newsletters, it makes us stand out from the agencies that just send a newsletter full of the properties on their books. Some people might consider this a distraction from the business, but to me it's a core part of our brand and our personality – it's who we are and it's an example of how we challenge in our space.

Our content creation is like the secret sauce for our brand, because we consistently produce content which aims to be helpful, whether that's our webinars, our newsletter or our social media posts. We align all of it around our personality of being helpful experts – I'll comment on new property legislation in the national or local media, and I'll explain what that legislation means for our customers in a piece for our newsletter, for example. Marketing is hugely important for a challenger brand, because it's how you ensure your message and your brand are consistently seen and heard. I can't stress enough how important consistency and repetition of your message and values are when you're a challenger brand. It can help to

131

think of it like going to the gym – you're not going to build muscle or lose fat overnight, it happens over a period of time as long as you're consistent.

If you want to be a challenger brand, look at ways of standing out. Start a podcast, start making agent-led videos, comment on the market in your content, do radio interviews, write articles for your local paper. There is so much you can do to stand out. Remember once you decide to do this, you need to be consistent. You will also need to continue doing it, especially when you are really busy.

To excel as a challenger brand, you need to surround yourself with inspiration. A lot of mine and Maria's inspiration these days comes from the mastermind group run by Sanjay which we joined during the Covid-19 pandemic. Each week we heard talks from the best of the best in the world of estate agency, and these people gave us ideas as well as motivating us to keep improving what we're doing. Wherever you are in your business journey, whether you're just starting out or have been going for over 26 years like us, you need to have that motivation to keep challenging – it's like my boxing match, I needed the stamina to keep going every round. If you can't find a estate agency mastermind group, why not set one up

Chapter 5: Be a Challenger

yourself? Find people you admire and like, have a diverse group who will share and help you. You in turn can help them.

When you're challenging the status quo, you also have to let go of what others think. Even in those moments of doubt (I still have them, even now) you need to find the courage to plough on when you know you're doing the right thing. You can't worry about what other people are saying about you, because this is your journey of continuous improvement. You have to do what's right for you and your business. People will always judge you, regardless of what you say or do. You have to accept that because it's part of life. There will always be haters out there, and you can't change them.

As I mentioned in the Introduction Lisa Novak has the best response to the haters: "Change the channel honey!" During a coaching session I had with her, she told me that she'd had people laughing at her, insulting her and then even copying her. She said there would be times when we'd wonder if anyone was even watching our videos, but that we needed to be consistent. I took that information on board and everything she said happened – but knowing that Lisa had also been through this gave us confidence that we were on the right track and

133

didn't require other people's approval if we wanted to stand out.

If you're ever unsure about what to say or do, come back to your vision, mission and values. Ask yourself, is this the right messaging? Is it helpful for my audience? Is it in the right tone for the people I want to speak to? It's also essential to make sure that any information you're sharing is correct – you need a strong foundation on which to build a challenger brand. When I forget this Paula, our marketing consultant, reminds me of our purpose and vision.

As I'm writing this, there is a lot of very controversial debate in Ireland about eviction bans. People are angry and upset. It's something I've spoken about publicly, but because I'm speaking as an expert it's vital that my information is correct. I check everything and I take advice from other professionals who know more about issues like this than me. If someone asks me to speak about something that is completely outside of my expertise, I'll just say no because I know that I need to stay in my lane.

If you're feeling nervous about putting yourself out there and stepping into this space as a challenger, just look around at the

Chapter 5: Be a Challenger

other people in your industry who are challenging success-fully – in estate agencies the people who stand out for me are Josh Tesolin and Lisa Novak, who are both in Australia. They have strong brands, they put themselves out there and they're consistently sharing their message and story. They don't worry about being judged, they just keep doing what they're doing. A saying I love is "Success leaves a trail", so look for others who you consider successful and see what you can learn from their trail.

WHY BECOMING A CHALLENGER WILL BOOST YOUR BUSINESS

In the modern world, where our attention spans are getting shorter and shorter, and businesses are creating more content than ever before, it's essential to find a way to stand out from the crowd and rise up above all of the noise. Even though social media and other online channels have given us more ways to reach our customers, they also mean that each and every one of us is constantly bombarded with information. In this world, you either blend in and get lost, or stand out and get seen.

But don't forget that you're not just competing for people's attention with other estate agents – you're competing with brands and influencers from every industry from health and fitness to food and psychology. This is why it's so important that you carve out a niche, find your tribe and then build a community. This is how you build relationships with your clients. At a deep psychological level, we can't tell the difference between knowing someone online and offline, so even if you've never met someone you will still feel as though you know them. This builds trust, which is important for all of us, but especially in business. It's KLT. Know, Like and Trust is so important for your customers when they think of you.

When you step into the challenger mentality, you're not going against your natural instincts, you're leaning into them. It's important that you're authentic to yourself throughout this process. That doesn't mean you won't have to do things that push you out of your comfort zone, but when those activities align with you and your values, you'll find the courage to do them anyway and that will make you stand out. It will also allow you to seize opportunities to grow your business and get ahead by doing so – you're not following everyone else's lead, you're forging your own path.

If you are finding it difficult to get out of the day-to-day activities and figure out how you can stand out from your

Chapter 5: Be a Challenger

competitors, you should focus on being your local expert and authority. Your local paper is always looking for content. Why not offer to submit a monthly market update? You can use this content across all of your social media platforms making sure the paper gets first copy. You can then repurpose that content on a newsletter. All of this requires an investment of your time, but it does work. I have learnt that what I do today delivers results in three to six months' time and sometimes it takes a lot longer to reap the rewards. If you commit to providing a monthly market update, then you have to make sure you deliver. Then use that content for video and put out your monthly property market update on video. If you don't have a newsletter database, start one. You should be communicating and staying in touch with your clients at least once a month.

You need to build a nurture journey and stay in touch with your clients. This will require a system and a process. You will need a good customer relationship management (CRM) technology system. The key thing to remember is that your clients need to have you in mind when they need to sell or rent their property. Figure out your own stay in touch policy. This could include market updates, industry news, interior design tips or a more up-to-date valuation offer for their home. Better still, send a birthday or an anniversary card.

Steps for success

- Constantly promote yourself and your business – marketing is the lifeblood of your business.

- Align your messaging to your mission, values and brand personality.

- Seek out people you admire – who can you look to for inspiration?

- Be consistent – put yourself out there every day, week, month and create a marketing plan that you can follow.

CHAPTER 6

DEVELOP YOUR TRIBE

As we all know, leading a business is not a journey you embark on alone. You have a bus full of people along for the ride, and you need these people to be able to keep up with your business as it evolves and grows. In Chapter 3 I talked about finding the right people for your bus, but you can't stop with hiring. You have to help these people develop their skills and grow their knowledge.

Development means different things to different people and, if you Google the term, you'll come up with various definitions. There are two that particularly resonate with me though:

gradual advancement or *growth*. Continuous improvement is a cornerstone of our business and something I personally believe in, as you'll have gathered by now.

DEVELOPMENT STARTS WITH YOU

It's only through continuous improvement that you can build a high-performing team, but this approach starts with one person – the boss (you). You need to continually improve if you're going to be an effective leader.

As the leader, it's your role to set the tone. To really commit to people development you have to develop yourself first – without external input, how are you going to know what good looks like? This is why having mentors is so important because then you can learn from people who are better at certain aspects of business than you. I admit that I don't read enough, but I love listening to industry podcasts, such as *The World Class Agency, The Other Hand, Normal Gets You Nowhere* and *Diary of a CEO and The Tom Ferry Podcast Experience*.

I'm always working to develop myself, whether that's reading a book, going to the gym, participating in a mastermind group or

Chapter 6: Develop Your Tribe

travelling to estate agency conferences where I can hear from people I respect and admire. I want to continuously improve the service we deliver and continuously deliver growth within the business. To do this I have to develop and then take what I learn and apply it in my business to help my team to develop too. I also love meeting people who attend these events. I get a huge buzz out of it and feel super-charged when I get back. The team often laughs and says things like "I wonder what Regina will come back with this time."

For example, in 2022, Maria came with me to a marketing conference in London. We went with Sanjay and six others from his mastermind group. It was an amazing few days and we made some significant changes to the business after that trip – in fact, I'd say we learnt more from our industry peers in the cab rides and over dinner than from the conference itself. It was right after that trip that we decided to hire a virtual assistant and we've since hired a second – so now we have two full-time team members who are based in South Africa. We also changed our entire accounts process by outsourcing most of our accounts to an accountancy firm as a result of conversations with others on that trip. We've saved a lot of money and improved how we do things – it's a good reminder to look at how we do things and see how we can do them smarter, faster or better, and that an outside set of eyes can potentially point out better ways of working.

As a business owner, I know how challenging and tiring it can be to keep focusing on continuous improvement. We're always busy; there is always a huge list of stuff to do; we're always working on sharpening the saw, as Stephen R. Covey puts it, which simply means keeping our skills at the cutting edge.

COACHING VERSUS TELLING

Developing yourself is one thing – the other equally important part of the equation is developing your people. To help everyone on your team develop, it's important to have a coaching mindset, rather than simply telling people what to do and expecting them to do it. I know that it can feel like the easy option is to tell someone what to do, but in the long term you will see better results and have a more capable and engaged team if you can get into the habit of coaching them so that they see where they need to improve and understand why it's important for them to do so.

Chapter 6: Develop Your Tribe

Coaching questions are especially important when someone screws up. Instead of getting angry and telling them how to fix the issue, pause and ask yourself, "How can I help them see how this went wrong?" It's all about finding the learning point in an experience and helping the other person to reach that same conclusion.

For example, while I was writing this book a member of my team made a mistake with a report that was sent to a client who has a sizable portfolio with us. He had asked for a report containing the figures for the rent, maintenance and other expenses on his portfolio, covering 2021 to the most recent complete month in 2023. I saw that the report had been sent to him, but when I checked it I noticed it only contained the figures for 2022. I was frustrated, but I wanted this member of the team to learn the importance of checking reports like this before they are sent to the client.

Instead of telling him what was wrong, I asked a series of questions to help him uncover where in the process things had fallen down. I asked whether he'd read what the client had asked for, to which he replied he had. Then I asked if he'd read the report that was sent in before it was passed onto the client – as he answered with "no", I could see he had grasped the importance of checking reports like this rather than simply forwarding them on.

We talked a little more about the situation in relation to our mission of bringing happiness to our staff, customers and community; and we discussed how if we take pride in what we do, we need to focus on getting it right the first time.

This particular situation created a lot more work and, obviously, the client was disappointed not to receive all the information he needed in the first instance. But the team member in question learned a valuable lesson and I don't think they'll make the same mistake in the future.

I know I keep referring to our mission and values, but they truly do steer everything we do within the business. When everyone on your team is clear about the company's mission and values, it makes it much easier to have these difficult conversations and remove the emotion from them, which means it doesn't come across as personal or as though you are picking on them.

Chapter 6: Develop Your Tribe

TRAINING:
MORE THAN JUST AN INDUCTION

Our mission statement and values are included in our online training system, which is hosted on Trainual, and we encourage everyone on the team to refer back to these resources whenever they need to. It isn't just a training process that you work through when you start at Liberty Blue and then forget, it's a set of resources that every member of our team can use in their work every day to guide them towards the right decisions that are aligned with our mission and values.

That said, we now refer to our mission and our values in daily morning meetings, and we have the mission and values in a frame in the office. We've since put our values in reception too. They need to take centre stage and everyone needs to live the values and mission for them to really be effective. Having our mission and values on Trainual isn't enough – they have to be talked about. One of the two values that come up daily are "we do the right thing" and "we take pride in what we do". If photos in property adverts aren't up to standard we can refer to taking pride in what we do and it becomes about being consistent and having a standard. People then don't take it personally when you have to check them. In a difficult HR decision, it's easy to figure out what to do when you know "that you do the right thing", whatever that might mean. You do the right thing by the employee and by the company. It's a great compass to guide each one of us. I remember one of the team pulling me up and saying, "Regina that's not the right thing to do." Immediately I said, "Actually, you are so right." When this kind of thing happens, you know that everyone is living the business' values.

Absolutely every process and system in your business should be documented and uploaded into your training CRM, whether you use Trainual or another platform. This kind of platform works well for both onboarding new team members and up-skilling your existing members of staff. In recent times, we have started recording our training on video and this really helps with onboarding new people as well as saving a lot of time. We use Loom – it's a great resource, check it out.

We are regulated by the property regulator in Ireland, and as a result every person on our team has to complete a certain number of hours of continuing professional development (CPD) each year. The regulator runs courses around estate agencies, property legislation and best practice in the industry which makes it very valuable for our team.

Chapter 6: Develop Your Tribe

There are also government support bodies in Ireland (and I'm sure it's the same elsewhere) that offer free or low-cost training and resources in a host of areas related to business. If anyone on my team goes on a course, I ask them to email over their notes, as well as a list of actions they are going to take as a result of what they have learned.

Encouraging everyone to implement what they learn is the hard part. This is why it's so important to ask people to set actionable outcomes from any training they receive. Even having just one thing that they're going to implement is better than nothing. Sanjay often says, "There is shelf development or self development." How many times have you gone to an event or training session, thought it was great, but then didn't actually implement what you learnt?

Training doesn't have to be a formal course – it can also mean attending lunchtime networking events in your local area. For example, Darragh from our office regularly attends local "lunchtime bite" events, where people from various Waterford businesses meet up, have lunch and listen to an expert talk. By regularly attending these, he's always learning something new and he's getting to network with our local community too. I ask him to create content for our social media channels while he's there as well. The point is, training doesn't always have to be super formal or take up days of an employee's time. It can be something short and sweet – and no less effective as a result. Attending events like this is also a great networking opportunity. As estate agents, we are meeting prospective clients everywhere.

We also use a skills matrix to see what skills we have within the business and where we could upskill people on the team. Our aim is to help everyone be as confident as possible in as many areas of the business as possible, and to ensure that there is consistency in terms of how we deal with our customers. It might sound trivial, but we make sure we all answer the phone in the same way so that every person who phones our office receives the same experience. It's this consistency that helps build your business' reputation.

Using a skills matrix can also help you identify individual components in someone's job that they are less comfortable with and identify areas where they would benefit from some additional training. Often these will be elements that are indirectly linked to their role, but they are still skills gaps that need to be addressed.

Chapter 6: Develop Your Tribe

I would like to give credit to my mentor, John Paul in the UK, for introducing me to the skills matrix. He coached me for over six months and this was one of the key things I took away from our time together, along with the importance of doing weekly/ bi-weekly one-to-ones with your team.

Creating your own skills matrix

To create a skills matrix, you break down the various tasks or steps that make up one element of someone's job to help you identify the areas where they may need more support. Let's take leading letting viewings as an example.

Ask what skills and knowledge will be needed for someone to become good at leading a letting viewing. This could include the process around the viewing itself, how to complete the Property Services Agreement with the client, and sales negotiations. You put each of these steps into your skills matrix for that task.

Next give the member of your team an overall score out of five, with one being weak and five being excellent, for leading letting viewings. Now give them a score for each of the

---

components you've identified that make a good letting viewing. This will help you identify which area (or areas) this person needs more training in. Obviously if they're new to your team, they are likely to start with a very low overall score, but as they complete their training and lead more letting viewings, you should see their scores increase.

This is a template skills matrix to get you started:

Behaviours	Score	Performance Level
1		
2		
3		
Key Activities (Linked to KPIs)	Score	Performance Level
1		
2		
3		
Identify development needs (refer to skills)		
SMART goals for development acitivites		
Review and evaluation of last session		

1 = Underperforming	2 = Developing
3 = Performing	4 = Exceeding

Chapter 6: Develop Your Tribe

The skills matrix is also a useful tool for identifying areas of your business where there could be a weakness, such as if there's a task that only one member of your team knows how to do. For example, we had a situation where a VIP client was told that it would take a full week for one of his rental properties to be inspected after the tenants moved out. The client, understandably, wasn't happy. In actual fact, the inspection was completed within a day, but my team member had been unsure of the inspector's availability so had gone with the idea of "underpromise, overdeliver".

In this instance, the client was very unhappy. But it also highlighted a training need – we only had one subcontractor who could do the move out inspections for our clients. By the time I became involved, my new manager John (who I'll talk more about shortly) had already identified the gap and booked a training session on move out inspections for other members of the team.

Whenever you're filling in a skills matrix for your business, think about what is required to fulfil the business' needs and how many people on your team are capable of completing each task. The more you are able to develop each individual's skills, the better it will be for your business because it will mean you can more easily cover absence, whether planned like a holiday or unplanned like sickness, and redeploy resources to where they're needed most. More importantly, you can then use your key and senior people who have the highest value and skills to do the most important work. Look at having your junior people do the more basic tasks, especially around administration. I see this as leveraging your human resources.

This is something that is important and not necessarily urgent, but the more we invest in the important, not urgent stuff, the more likely we are to prevent things from becoming urgent. For example, a second and third person being trained up in property inspections or doing up contracts means if someone goes out sick or leaves you have a back-up plan. This is something I've learnt the hard way. Our two team members based in South Africa can now answer the telephones. This means if we have to close the office or someone on reception is out sick, the business still functions seamlessly.

Chapter 6: Develop Your Tribe

FEEDBACK DRIVES CONTINUOUS IMPROVEMENT

Training for your team also comes into the conversations you have with them on a daily and weekly basis, in the form of feedback. Each person on our team has a bi-weekly one-to-one with their manager and this is an opportunity for them to reflect on what's gone well and what hasn't gone so well over the past two weeks. It's important to ask those questions and let them lead the conversation initially.

The questions we ask include, what do you think went well for you? What didn't go so well? This would also be a good time to mention an issue or a few issues during the last couple of weeks. Use the one-to-one space as an opportunity to address areas for improvement or to have those straight-talking conversations, rather than nit-picking every little mistake when it comes up.

If, as their manager, you've noticed mistakes or any areas for improvement throughout the weeks, you can then share your feedback with them in a constructive way during those meetings. It often helps if you start by saying, "Can I give you some feedback?" because then you frame the conversation around the idea of continuous improvement. If you're worried about forgetting small things, you could jot down notes on your phone every day so you have your topics for discussion.

Your one-to-ones are a chance to help people course correct before they go too far off the rails. They are really important for performance management and they help your team manage their expectations in line with yours. If you don't tell someone they're doing a bad job for six months, and then all of a sudden tell them they haven't passed their probationary period as a result, it's as though you've thrown a grenade at them and walked away. That's not fair, so you need to have these regular conversations to make sure you are both on the same page and that the other person understands where they need to improve as well as the consequences of not doing so.

Being supportive in these conversations is the key. Ask for your team member's opinion about the issues you're raising. Offer them more training if you or they identify this as a possible solution. Make sure each member of your team feels valued. Listen to what they're telling you so that you can understand what areas they might need help with, but also what areas they're doing well in. Celebrate the wins and include the positives. It's important to keep your team motivated.

Chapter 6: Develop Your Tribe

Sometimes you will need to have uncomfortable conversations with people on your team, and even though I have gotten better at having these conversations over the years, they still aren't pleasant. But they are necessary because problems don't go away if you ignore them, they actually grow if you don't deal with them. To be an effective leader, you need to be supportive and coach your team, but you also need to be direct and draw their attention to what needs to be improved.

Ultimately a one-to-one is a safe space to help people grow and be the best versions of themselves. I promise you that the more you do this the more comfortable you get with it. Your team will appreciate the one-to-one time and it's also an opportunity for them to get stuff off their chest. Maybe as the manager or boss you might need feedback around your behaviours? This is a good thing as when things fester they grow into bigger issues.

The key to making these conversations easier for you and the people on your team is to have them consistently and to make sure there is clarity about what these conversations will cover. No one should go into one of these meetings and be surprised by what's discussed.

John and I worked with Gemma Noonan, who heads up Matt Giggs' residential estate agency businesses, to improve in this area. She taught us something really important – not to focus on every issue at the time it happens. She said, "Regina, John, don't be pulling people up every time they make a mistake or drop the ball or there is an issue. Try to bunch it together for a discussion during your one-to-one." Our job is to motivate people and hold them accountable. In order to do that, we need to approach feedback in a way that gets the best result for them and for the business. Admittedly I have to check myself – I am a bit of a perfectionist which isn't really that good a thing sometimes. So when I see something I'm not happy with in the business, I try to hold back and mention it to John for when he is doing his one-to-one with that person. After all, our mission is to bring happiness to our colleagues. That is something I am very aware of, and I can hear Gemma in my ear.

The one-to-one is also an opportunity to see how the other person's week is going. What is going well and what hasn't gone so well. I like to role play and play out how to deal with difficult situations, and I find that people really learn well from this.

Chapter 6: Develop Your Tribe

ACCOUNTABILITY:
THE SECRET SAUCE FOR DEVELOPMENT

All of us need accountability to make sure we take action based on what we learn. When it comes to providing that accountability within your business, what I've learned is that when you hold people accountable, they will either embrace it and improve or they will get off your bus. If they do the latter, then they weren't the right person to be part of your team in the first place.

Within Liberty Blue, each one of us has a set of key performance indicators (KPIs), and we review these in each bi-weekly one-to-one. For example, let's imagine one of my team has to make sure that 350 oil and gas boilers are serviced each year. They have a KPI of booking ten boiler services per week. At their next one-to-one, you check the system and can see that they've only booked two boiler services that week.

The conversation could go like this:

"I can see you've only booked two boiler services this week, can you tell me what happened?"

"If you recall, Regina, you gave me a huge project and asked me to pause the boiler services this week so that I could take that on."

"You're right, of course. Let's make a note of that."

By asking your team member to explain what happened you are holding them accountable for their actions. They may have a good reason for not having hit that KPI, in which case it is important to record this so you are both aware of the situation when you next meet. But one thing you can be sure of is that if you're asking them about their KPIs in your bi-weekly one-to-ones, they won't forget about them.

As another example, our Property Service Agreements (PSAs) expire after five years, so the person in charge of sending out the new ones with our new terms and increased fees has a target. It's one thing to send out the contracts, but we also have to make sure they come back signed. The one-to-one is an ideal place to establish if the KPIs are on target and if not, why and what can we do about this?

Some people might say they don't have time to do it – I would say we don't have time not to. In all my 26 years in business I

Chapter 6: Develop Your Tribe

have learnt what doesn't get checked doesn't get done. KPIs are brilliant, but unless you check in on them, measure progress and discuss them on a weekly and bi-weekly basis, there is a good chance that these things won't get done because that is human nature. It's also important that the KPIs you set for your team have a bit of a stretch to them. They need to be above and beyond turning up and doing the basic job if you want to cultivate a business where everyone has a growth mindset and therefore build a business that will grow and thrive without requiring continuous input from you.

Another KPI for one of the team is the maintenance tasks open and outstanding on Fixflo. This is an important metric to measure. Having good technology has stood us very well in business and this type of technology helps us to eliminate, automate and reduce activities. We learnt about this system, the problems it solves for agents and how it improves client experience when we went to Base Properties in London – owned by Kristjan the Viking who I mentioned in Chapter 1. Hopefully you can see that by having peers to learn from who help you step up your business, clarity around how you do things (eliminate, automate, reduce), and bi-weekly one-to-ones, you build a culture of innovation and accountability.

Within our industry it's particularly important that everyone does what is required for compliance, because there are a lot of regulations we have to adhere to in Ireland – of course it's no different in the likes of the UK, US or Australia. As an example, when a sale closes the seller's solicitor will email us to tell us we can release the keys and this email then needs to be saved on file. To ensure we are complying with these regulations, I've asked my manager John to carry out regular audits of the team's work.

The first time we did this, we discovered that not all of those emails from the solicitors were being saved immediately. This means John can discuss this with the relevant team members in their one-to-ones, and then John and I discuss the overall findings of the audits he's carried out in his one-to-one with me.

This simply highlights the importance of having regular one-to-ones with each person on your team. When you do, these kinds of things become part of the regular conversation and it is much easier to hold individuals accountable for doing these essential parts of their roles. After each of his one-to-ones, John sends an email summarising the conversation and listing what that person needs to work on or any actions agreed. In

Chapter 6: Develop Your Tribe

their next one-to-one, they can review those notes and make sure nothing has slipped through the cracks.

The other tool we have found to be a game changer is a daily morning meeting with the whole team. These are a chance for all of us to come together, say what we're working on and discuss any challenges we might be facing with the rest of the team. They've been incredibly helpful for improving communication between everyone on the team and have made sure that everyone knows the plan for the day, which helps the business run more efficiently. These meetings have also helped everyone bond better, and are a way of improving our work relationships.

INVEST IN YOUR TEAM

There are several ways in which you can invest in your team. The first is probably the most obvious – by hiring new people into roles and growing your team. Hiring someone isn't necessarily an investment in the person though, in fact it's more an investment in the business. The way you invest in the people you bring in is through the training and support you provide them with.

One thing that we learned from our mentor Gemma Noonan is that if we're going to hold people accountable, we need to give them a proper training plan, the right tools for the job, as well as be clear about our expectations. This is what we have done for our general manager John and it's been enormously fruitful.

When we hired John as the manager in our business, we knew he was moving into a new industry and that this could be challenging for him, so we hired a mentor for him. This mentor, whose name is Tony, is the former general manager of a large multinational corporation. Tony was already on our bus and was heavily involved in the recruitment process, so it felt natural for him to be John's mentor and provide additional support that I'm not able to. Tony is available whenever John needs him. John has told us how valuable this support has been for him, and how it has helped him be more measured in how he deals with situations that arise. Providing a mentor is one of the ways we delivered security and showed commitment to John in his role. But it has also allowed us to bring the best out of the people on our team.

Tony's role isn't just limited to being John's mentor – he supports us with the recruitment process and conducts exit interviews when people leave the business. As someone external,

Chapter 6: Develop Your Tribe

he's able to gather great feedback and help us learn and evolve within the business. He recently worked closely with John on putting together an entire stills matrix for every element and activity within the business.

We knew we couldn't afford to not have a manager for much longer, and now that John's settling in we can see how much more he'll be able to take on in time, which will in turn allow us to grow and develop the business even further. But this growth in the business started with investing in our people. They are your company's most important and valuable resource.

By hiring a manager with a financial background, we have invested in the future of the business. I can tell you in the first nine months since John started, he has contributed enormously to the business. Financially we have improved our bottom line, he has brought business in and he has hugely contributed to the overall happiness within the business. He has a brilliant sense of humour. Many business owners see hiring a manager as an expense, but I see it as a valuable investment and in this case one that's paying off.

We have also asked John for his feedback about what he's felt has worked particularly well for him since he started with us.

We have provided him with a lot of support, definitely a lot more than we ever did with the other managers we've hired in the past. Although John is incredibly high calibre and has a passion for property, this is the first time he's ever worked in the estate agency business. I coached him for 30 minutes every morning in the first six months he was with the business, helping him work through different scenarios that he was encountering in the business.

One of the most important aspects of this was coaching around how to respond to situations as a leader, because we set the scene for everybody else. That means we can't panic when something goes wrong, we have to be calm and take control. Think of this like being the captain of a ship when there's water coming in. You can't panic. You have to give commands like "lower the lifeboats" and encourage everyone else to behave calmly. While we don't have a sinking ship, we do sometimes have to deal with difficult clients and we do have to solve problems, sometimes big ones. I've learned that resilience is an essential tool for facing adversity and challenges.

When you face a big problem, you have to ask yourself questions like, "Have I any control over it?", "How can I break this down?" and "Why did it happen and can I stop it from

Chapter 6: Develop Your Tribe

happening again?" More often than not, when something goes wrong the person who has been affected wants to know why things went wrong and that you'll take steps to prevent the same issue from happening again. When you think about these questions before having that conversation, you're in a much better position to speak to a client or a colleague about the situation and remain calm.

RESILIENCE: AN ESSENTIAL TOOL

Developing resilience is something we all need to do, no matter our job, and it's something that we need to take personal responsibility for. We have to look after ourselves, which means eating well, getting enough sleep and doing exercise. As an employer, I can't control that for every member of my team, but what I can do is provide a wellness programme that helps educate everyone on my team about how to set themselves up for success.

I engaged a great lady called Calodagh McCumiskey from Spiritual Earth to run a number of in-person sessions over a period of time. The title was "Set yourself up for Success" and

Calodagh covered the 12 pillars of wellbeing. She talked about stress and how to set yourself up for peak performance. It was super interesting.

The pillars of wellbeing are our physical, mental, emotional, creative, social, financial, spiritual, environmental, digital, communication, relationships, and sense of purpose. By talking and sharing stories, the team became a lot more aware of the importance of self-care. We learnt a lot about how the mind works. Did you know that the mind has between 50,000 and 70,000 thoughts per day?! When we fight things in our mind, we create stress in our bodies, but 90 per cent of thoughts are repetition. Switching off and relaxation practice is so important for all of us.

REMEMBER: If you want your life to change, what has to change is me. Thanks Calodagh for these important tips.

Tips for improving your wellbeing

- Assess where you are. How are your pillars of wellbeing?

- Face your stresses and convert them to strengths.

Chapter 6: Develop Your Tribe

- Quality rest and relaxation every day!!

- To set yourself up for success, start your day WELL! The first hour is key. What are you saying to yourself?

- What does it take for you to have a great day? Exercise? Food? Connection? Fun? Integrate whatever you come up with into each day.

- What area do you want to achieve success in?

- What habitually causes stress? Notice the patterns and design a life with a minimum of unhealthy stress.

- The best way to predict the future is to create it.

- Be... Learn... Do... Visualise... Create.... Reflect... and repeat.

The other way in which I support my team to become more resilient is by acknowledging the wins, building people up and having their backs. I've always made it very clear that if a client is rude or treats anyone on the team badly, I won't tolerate that.

I want everyone on my team to feel safe, because that is very important for developing resilience, particularly in our industry.

Within this business, this is vital because not everyone will be happy all of the time – especially when you have a business with a large maintenance side to it like ours. Often you have to ring a client to tell them that the washing machine in their property has broken down and that they will need to pay for it to be repaired – you're not going to phone them to tell them it's flying like a bird! Many of our landlords understand that this is just part of renting properties, but some of them can be unreasonable at times and this is when it's so important for my team to know that I've got their back. This knowledge helps them to be resilient in the face of an unreasonable customer.

As an example, we were dealing with a client for the last eight years, he had 10 properties and the fees were valuable to the business. However, as each year went on so did his demands. He refused to pay administration charges that were additional to our monthly fees. He paid less than everyone else and demanded a much higher service. As his demands grew, the happiness within the team dropped. A level of fear by two of our best people kicked in. So when this client demanded lower fees again, I said sorry but we can't reduce our fees and knew

Chapter 6: Develop Your Tribe

he would leave. He did, and when we look at the amount of time he consumed and the fear he created during our interactions it was a good thing to say goodbye to his business. The older I get and the longer I am in business, the more I believe it is hugely important to have positive relationships in order to be happy. So happiness in my business is a very important element of our success – after all, we are not for everyone (a valuable mantra I got from Sanjay).

Knowing that there is a process to follow and providing everyone on the team with training about how to deal with difficult clients is also essential. This means they'll have the tools to potentially calm the other person down, but also the presence of mind to understand that if they can't resolve the issue then the landlord's reaction is out of their control, and that both myself and the rest of the management team will support them in dealing with this difficult client.

Resilience also comes from knowing that if you're sick, you can take time off and rest; if you need more training in a specific area that you can ask for it; if you need support from a colleague that you can ask.

When your team isn't resilient, they're not set up for success. They are much more likely to take things personally. In the face of an unreasonable client, they may become angry, meet the other person's anger with a similar response and in doing so blow the situation out of proportion. Anger also causes our bodies to tense up and release cortisol, which increases our stress levels. When we're stressed, we're not happy and what often happens is that we expend a great deal of energy on a situation that doesn't warrant it. This means it's not an effective use of time or money for the business. Building a resilient team will, therefore, have many positive benefits for your business – happier clients, happier staff, more efficient operations and less stress for everyone.

CHANGE IS INEVITABLE

Change is part of life, it's part of business and it's vital for continuous improvement. As a business owner, you have to make sure you're always questioning what you do to see if there's a better, more efficient way of approaching a task. The longer you've been in business, the easier it is to become stuck in your ways and to simply do things the way they have always been done.

Chapter 6: Develop Your Tribe

I've said already that mentors are important people to have on your bus because they can help you see what good really looks like. I'm always looking at how we can learn from our mentors in the estate agency industry to find out how they do things – can we adopt similar practices and improve the efficiency in our business?

For example, we have started working with two virtual assistants (VAs) in South Africa after hearing about how this has dramatically improved the efficiency of rent payments for one of our colleagues in Sanjay's mastermind – Fran from Moss Mentors. She made a comment about having done all the rent payments for the business in an hour from a hotel room while we were at a marketing conference. It stopped me in my tracks. Our rent payments seem to take over a week! I asked how she managed that, which is when I learned about the high calibre VAs who are based in South Africa. They have industry experience and they're all team players – and they can streamline the process significantly.

Maria, who was with me at the time, was sold on the idea once she'd heard Fran talking about it, so we took this back to John who has since implemented it. Lianna, our South Africa-based VA, posts the rents and John then only has to spend one hour twice a month making the bank transfers. Through our conversation with Fran we also discovered the way in which we'd been handling bank transfers was hugely inefficient, so we have made changes here too.

The danger with being in business for 26 years is that you can get stuck in routines and processes that aren't the best way of doing things. By developing ourselves as business leaders, Maria and I have learned, and are still very much learning, what good can look like, and have made positive changes in our business as a result. This is why it's so important to question everything you do on a regular basis.

This conversation made us scrutinise other areas of the business and when we looked, we found huge inefficiencies elsewhere as well. For instance, one member of the team was printing off and filing every statement. Not only is this not good for the environment, it's also a ferocious waste of time and it eats up a lot of space. But we weren't even aware it was happening. Now that we or should I say John has seen the inefficiency, we have created a new process and trained our team accordingly, making everyone's lives easier and improving the business' operations.

Chapter 6: Develop Your Tribe

Whilst it might appear that I and my business have got it all figured out, this is not the case. We are working on continuous improvement all the time. Only last week, I realised how important it is to go through the entire skills matrix – i.e. every task in the business – and make sure our training plan covers cross training for everyone. For example, we need more than one person in the business who can operate the matterport, floor plans and 360 tours. We need more than one person who can write property adverts. We have also restarted with internal audit checks of every process to ensure everyone is doing each task correctly and consistently. For example, how maintenance is logged, how the reporting to contractors is handled. Another very important check is compliance checks for lettings and sales, and ensuring that our digital files have all the information that is required by the property regulator. We don't want the drama of getting an audit letter from the regulator and not being up to date with everything that's required. Whilst it may appear mundane it's hugely important.

The key phrase to remember, and I'll come back to this in much more detail in the next chapter, is *automate, eliminate and reduce*. In relation to the rent payments, we could automate them using batch payments, we could eliminate printing and storing physical documents and in doing so reduce the time everyone spends on this task each month. We did all of this by embracing change.

Change is essential for the development of you, your team and your business. To cultivate that mindset of continuous improvement you need to embrace change, and so does everyone else who works for you. By helping everyone on your team develop a continuous improvement mindset, you are also training them to look for inefficiencies in your processes and systems, and suggest improvements.

Within the world of estate agencies this is particularly important because it can be so admin-heavy and, unless you have really good technology and systems, some of the work that goes on behind the scenes, that your team has to pick up, can be a desperate drag.

Of course, you may have people on your team who don't want to change the way you do things. These are the people who might tell you that something "can't" be done another way, even though you know of other organisations who do things differently. In these situations, it's important to push back. Ask your team to look at what those other organisations are doing and figure out how to do something similar in your business.

Chapter 6: Develop Your Tribe

At Liberty Blue this all plays into our tagline of *Smarter, Faster, Better.* We all want to live and work to these values, which means working smart, having efficient systems, approaching tasks with a sense of urgency and making sure we are looking at how we can continuously improve.

As well as evaluating your team and business processes for development opportunities, it's important to assess your suppliers as well. Sometimes when you are doing business with a company for a long time they can become complacent, so it is always worth looking at what else is available and whether there can be any improvement. For example, we recently changed our accountant, who has taught us new ways of using our accounting system Xero to save us time and physical resources like paper. We want everyone in the business, whether they are a member of the team or a supplier we work with, to have a solutions-focused mindset.

LOOK OUTSIDE YOUR BUSINESS FOR INSPIRATION

I've said it before and I'll say it again – mentors are invaluable for helping you to develop your business and your team.

If you're leading a business, I believe you need at least one mentor who can lift you outside of your day-to-day activity, show you what good can look like from a different perspective and bring enormous insights and learnings.

But development and good ideas don't only come from mentors. You can also fast-track your business by surrounding yourself with the right people from within the estate agency industry. For example, I often call John Kennedy who owns his own estate agency and software business and we chat for ages about technology and better ways of working. I'm also part of two estate agency mastermind groups and they have been invaluable for my business' development. If you don't have a group like this where you are, set one up. Even though I'm part of a mastermind, I've organised my own group in Ireland too.

In May 2023, I arranged for a group of five independent agents to come to the Liberty Blue offices for half a day of brainstorming and masterminding. It was an opportunity for us to share what's working in our businesses and get some input from others on any challenges we were facing. The key to these groups being effective is that you feel safe, can be vulnerable and open, and feel supported by the rest of the people who are involved.

Chapter 6: Develop Your Tribe

This comes back to what we all know as business owners – that we need to carve out time to spend *on* our businesses as well as in them. I know how much of a challenge this can be, but if you're only working in your business then you will only be serving its immediate needs, which means you'll have no pipeline and potentially no plan for how to generate business once what you're working on currently finishes. It's hugely important to develop your people throughout your journey. Growing your team and leveraging resources are critical to growing your business and creating capacity for you as the owner or manager to focus on your long term strategy.

Working on your business means having a future focus. While I was writing this book, we paid for the templates for six expert guides that we can then edit (they are UK-focused, so we needed to make them Irish-focused) and release. This content sits alongside our webinars and newsletters as part of our mission to be helpful experts. This is just one small part of our plan to help us stay in front of people and generate new leads, but it's important. It's also one thing to create leads from these guides, but another to follow up on them.

If you aren't providing guides and expert blogs, my advice is to start and start soon. This is an opportunity to create valuable leads for future business; leads that you can nurture and stay in touch with, for when they are ready to sell, as I mentioned earlier.

You need to phone the people who download the guides and see if you can help them on their journey. Previously, I used to make these calls, but now we have one person in the office who makes them. Within the next few months, we'll have three people who make these calls regularly – it's all part of growing different people's skills and looking at all of the activities that are required within the business to make it a success. Even on the days when I'm working in the business, I will always be thinking about how we can maximise what we're doing and use any content we're creating today, for tomorrow. Remember, the seeds we sow today will be the harvest we reap in the tomorrows.

YOU'RE NEVER TOO BUSY FOR TRAINING

As a business owner and leader, it can be easy to think you're "too busy for training". It's a rock we've all perished on I'm sure. But when you start providing consistent, structured training for your team and see the difference in both their performance

Chapter 6: Develop Your Tribe

and happiness levels, it becomes clear that it's a necessity not a "nice to have".

I've seen the benefits of investing time and energy into training through the progress of our manager John, and he's finding the same thing in his role. While I was writing this book, he went on a training course in the UK and his biggest takeaway was that he wasn't spending enough time training his new recruits. Since returning from that course, he's dedicated a lot more time to one new member of staff in particular, and in just weeks was reaping the rewards. She became better at her job, happier and more confident, all because he put time into training her and building a stronger relationship.

Steps for success

- Be consistent – development is an ongoing journey for everyone.

- Create a training plan – use a skills matrix to identify gaps, set clear KPIs, measure performance and have an online training resource.

- Find a group of peers or mastermind group – use this space to share ideas and problems. It's a super way to help you and your team to get better.

- Implement – put what you learn into practice and hold people accountable.

- Role play difficult situations with your team – the value of on the job training in various situations shouldn't be underestimated.

- Embrace change – try new things because this is how you grow.

CHAPTER 7

SYSTEMS AND PROCESSES

As I mentioned in the previous chapter, there are three key elements to creating systems and processes for your business: reduce, eliminate, automate. This is a concept that our coach Tony has drilled into me and the rest of the Liberty Blue team. But the reason these three simple words are so powerful is that when you focus on where you can reduce, eliminate and automate within your business, you can see significant improvements in your business efficiency, as well as the happiness of your staff and customers.

Harnessing technology is essential if you are to reduce, eliminate and automate in today's world. In Chapter 1 I told you the story of how Maria and I met Kristjan Byfield at a proptech conference in London, and how the time we spent with him and his team revolutionised our business. In this chapter, I'm going to take a deeper dive into the systems and processes you need for a successful estate agency business, and I'll share the key pieces of technology we use at Liberty Blue to reduce, eliminate and automate as much as possible.

Before we get into technology and systems it's important to "begin with the end in mind". Ask yourself what you want to achieve? What type of business do you want to own or run? What is your mission? Do you and your team have the right mindset to achieve what you want to achieve? Are you going to stay committed and consistent in order to achieve your goals no matter what challenges arise? Do you have the right people on your bus to get to where you want to go?

CUTTING OUT THE NOISE

Before I go into any of the specifics of what we changed, I would just like to take a moment to highlight the significant

Chapter 7: Systems and Processes

change in our office environment, which has come about due to all the technology we've introduced in recent years. Before we went about introducing the technology, the key thing for me was to begin with the end in mind. I knew our office environment needed to change – I didn't know where to start, but I did know that we needed to explore a better way of doing things. Having a mindset of continuous improvement is important for success and, of course, general happiness in the workplace.

Like many estate agents, our office never stopped. It was as though there was a revolving door of people coming in and out, whether people looking for homes to rent, landlords or even some of our contractors who carry out maintenance on the properties we manage. It was *always* noisy. The phones didn't stop ringing. There was a constant tapping in the background as people responded to dozens, if not hundreds, of emails every day. There was always a conversation happening somewhere.

When we visited Kristjan's office, the thing that struck me the most was the silence. It was almost eerily quiet and calm. No people rushing in and out. No phones ringing off the hook. Not even people rushing to reply to as many emails as possible.

From that day, I knew what I wanted the future to look like. I had absolute clarity: I wanted that kind of quiet, peaceful office environment.

My first piece of advice to you is to find someone successful whose business you admire and see what nuggets you can get from them. If you're lucky, you'll find yourself someone like Kristjan and his team, who were incredibly generous with their time. Once this person has shared some of their wisdom, it's your job to implement it. Take the action required to reap the rewards.

Fast forward four years from that meeting with Kristjan and our office is also calm and organised. We have achieved this by applying the reduce, eliminate, automate philosophy to everything we do and by introducing many of the pieces of technology we learned about from our visit to Kristjan's office. Across the team, we have developed a mindset of innovation and it's serving us well.

A mindset of innovation is one where we want to improve things and do things better. We don't want to be working on wasteful activities. When you create capacity by eliminating wasteful activities, you can do higher value activities. For

Chapter 7: Systems and Processes

example, having loads of emails going back and forth for communication with contractors and clients is wasteful. It's also hard to track. By saving time here, you can create time to work on marketing activities or making important client calls to connect with your customers.

The concept of reduce, eliminate, automate is embedded in our culture – we use it in team meetings to find smarter, faster and better ways of doing things. For example, in one recent team meeting I learned that a member of the team was replying manually to tenant applications via email. We came back to Tony's mantra of reduce, eliminate, automate. We knew we couldn't eliminate the emails, but the team quickly realised we could automate our responses with a simple auto-reply setting out the process, the situation and the next steps the person receiving that email would need to take. Not only does this save time, but it also adds value and there's no danger of someone not receiving a reply.

REDUCE

We use an app called InventoryBase to produce property inspection reports for our landlords. While we still go and inspect the property, the app significantly reduces the time this takes because when we upload photos into the app, it populates the information in a hugely detailed report that can then be passed onto the landlord. It's easy to train people to use and it means the report is consistent regardless of who carries out the inspection because there is a standard format.

PlanetVerify is another invaluable piece of software we use, which has significantly reduced the number of touchpoints we have with prospective tenants by providing a secure portal on which they can upload their references and ID. Technically this piece of technology could also fall into the "eliminate" category or the "automate" category, because it eliminates contact with unsuccessful tenants and has automated a great deal of the verification process.

This particular piece of software also ensures we are GDPR compliant, because it's no longer acceptable to ask prospective tenants to email over documents like ID and references. It's fully automated in that the tenants have to upload all of their documents, and they receive notifications from the software if anything is missing – no more phone calls chasing down references from our office!

Chapter 7: Systems and Processes

The software also allows you to "purge" people from the system if their application for a rental is unsuccessful, which is vital for maintaining GDPR compliance. It will also send them an automated response if we mark their application as unsuccessful, telling them that this is the case. This has significantly reduced the number of phone calls we receive asking about the progress of their application because they can see it all on the portal.

In the past, all the documentation was sent by email from the prospective tenants – can you imagine the volume of emails! In addition, when the person responsible for tenant references was sick, we didn't have access to the information. It was a hugely inefficient way of working.

Splink, an online payments system, has also helped us reduce touchpoints with tenants and landlords because it enables us to send a link requesting payment of an invoice, and the client can then pay online via the app. It's highly efficient and we no longer have the challenge of people phoning the office and giving their credit card details to us over the phone. Just imagine how the phones got clogged up, the length of the calls and the noise in the office – not to mention the frustration for the person at the end of the phone if we couldn't understand what they were saying – all of that is gone thanks to Splink.

ELIMINATE

We have eliminated people coming into our office to report maintenance issues by introducing a system called Fixflo. This piece of software allows tenants and landlords to report maintenance issues online, at a time that suits them. It is able to deal with 40 different languages and it features online tutorials for occupants about how to deal with problems like mildew in the bathroom, for example, that will likely be their responsibility to address rather than that of the landlord. We have recently uploaded video tutorials where the tenant can learn how to remedy the issue themselves. This saves time and money.

Our contractors also use Fixflo to provide updates on their progress with the various jobs logged in the portal. All of this means that maintenance issue reporting and repairs are now covered by a self-service system – our clients can report issues and check on the progress of the work at any time, without needing to wait to hear back from us. Albeit, we still need a

Chapter 7: Systems and Processes

person to manage the maintenance, Fixflo makes it considerably more efficient for everyone.

Another piece of tech that has proven invaluable is Offr, our online bidding platform for properties for sale. Prior to introducing Offr, we would have people texting and emailing us their bids, then we would have to go back and forth with the seller as well. To put in context just how much work this was, if we received 20 bids for a property that could amount to 120 touchpoints, not to mention additional phone calls and the fact that you're introducing the possibility of human error.

Now, bidders have to upload their documentation to the platform before they can make an offer, so we are pre-qualifying them. All the bidders and the seller can see the bids on the online platform, but these are anonymous to everyone but us, which means we remain GDPR compliant. They can also make an offer and check what other offers have been made 24/7, rather than having to wait for business hours to find out what's going on. Each time someone puts in a bid, everyone else bidding on that property gets a notification, which often leads to more bids being submitted and, therefore, a higher price for the sale. Buyers love the transparency, and that's really important for trust. The seller doesn't need to wait for updates from us either, as they can just log into their Offr account and see what's happening with their property.

One thing I learnt at Proptech London all those years ago is the importance of self-service platforms. Clients need to be able to access information when they want it 24/7, and the process needs to be transparent to build trust. I was recently bidding for a property with another agent on behalf of a family member and found the entire process slow – emails were sent and replies received only during business hours and there was no transparency around the other bidder. From a consumer perspective and in my view, it's old hat.

It also has significant benefits for our business. With this single piece of software, we have eliminated a huge amount of non-revenue-generating noise. We also use QR codes on our property listings to do the same with our rental properties, which has become particularly important at the time of writing when we have a housing crisis and, therefore, fewer properties available for rent. On our property listings, the lead photo is a QR code, which takes prospective tenants to a portal (PlanetVerify) where they can upload all of their information and documentation, again pre-qualifying them. If they don't

Chapter 7: Systems and Processes

do this, they receive an automated response telling them their application has been unsuccessful.

AUTOMATE

We reduced our costs significantly by outsourcing our accounts and this has also led to some fantastic savings in our time. The outsourcing of the accounts has been a game changer for the business. To give one simple example, rather than our contractors emailing the person in our accounts department each month, who would then print the invoices and file them, they now email accounts@libertyblue. The invoices sent here go straight to our accountants, who automatically upload them to Xero. This is an example of just one simple change that has reduced non-revenue-generating activity, improved efficiencies and reduced traffic to the office. Our manager John also gets a copy to authorise before he issues payment.

We also use a utility transfer company called Property Button to transfer all of the utilities for our rental properties when a tenant moves out, and we've been using an online system to allow clients to sign contracts for years.

Regina Mangan

USE SPOT CHECKS
TO KEEP EVERYONE ON TRACK

At the time of writing this book, we had just completed over 200 property inspections and were auditing the process to see where improvements could be made. Doing so showed us just how much time, resource and money goes into each of these inspections, so we have re-evaluated our fees and are now charging more for these services. Inspections in residential property management are essential as there can be serious consequences for our business as well as our clients if they aren't completed timely and correctly.

This process has also highlighted that in some places, corners were being cut, so we have now introduced regular audits of everyone's work to make sure we don't have a mammoth task of auditing everything in one go again. I'd like to stress that we haven't done everything perfectly in our business – we are always learning and improving along the way. This is one of those improvements.

Our manager John has a background in financial services, so I knew he'd be very good at making sure processes were followed, because of the nature of financial services. He now

Chapter 7: Systems and Processes

carries out weekly and monthly audits across all of our processes, paying particular attention to those that are required for compliance. Consistency is the key, and it's essential to physically check, and not just ask people, if things are being done by the book because, in my experience, people will often say that things are being done correctly even when they're not following the correct process. Remember – what gets checked gets done. Measurement and audits are not things I will ever leave to chance again.

Auditing the processes themselves, as well as people's work, has also allowed us to improve efficiencies. By doing so, John discovered that we were printing off all our monthly landlord statements and keeping them in a folder. I didn't realise this was happening, so didn't know it needed to be stopped. We have now updated our process so that these statements are saved on the client's file in our CRM system. We've eliminated the unnecessary expense and effort of physically printing everything; we've reduced the amount of space we need for document storage and we've eliminated the time required for someone to physically file the paperwork.

This might sound like a really small change, but believe me when I say it amounts to big savings, especially as we are legally required to keep all of this information for seven years.

When we audited our accounts processes we also discovered that some charges for work hadn't been applied to our office account, even though we had paid for the work. We discovered other things that should have been done that weren't being done. All of us are so busy in business we can forget the importance of internal controls and checks. This is an issue across many businesses and one we will work on to ensure it never happens again. Having a manager with strong financial savviness is already proving smarter. John came up with the idea to engage Debbie, who is based in the UK, to do a lot of regular audit compliance checks. I met Debbie at Proptec in London all those years ago and we stayed in touch. She's a real guru when it comes to property technology and systems and processes. She recently did a big clean up on duplicate property listings on FixFlo and training with the team and is another great person we have on our bus.

Chapter 7: Systems and Processes

TIME IS OUR MOST VALUABLE COMMODITY

It's well known that time is our most valuable commodity, whoever we are, because we can never get it back. Time is also the most wasted resource in business. There is no silver bullet to save time, but having the reduce, eliminate, automate mindset will certainly help. When you apply this to all the processes and systems in your business, it's not only time that you're saving for yourself and your team, but also for your clients.

Just imagine for a moment how much time it takes someone to come into your office to get the information they need. They need to make sure they come to the office during the hours you're open, which isn't always easy. There's the time and energy dedicated to travelling there, not to mention that when you pop into an office you're much more likely to stick around and have a chat rather than simply get what you need and go. Of course, this has an effect on your staff's time too, because they have to engage with the customer and potentially take time searching for what they need.

Now think about how much simpler and quicker it is when you have information on an online system that anyone can access at a time that suits them. It's far more efficient from everyone's perspective and it's infinitely more convenient. You can fit submitting documents or references around work, picking up children from school or anything else you might do in your daily life.

As if to highlight how hideously inefficient visiting the office is, a man recently came in to collect a reference. He asked for it to be printed, so one of the members of my team attempted to do so, only to find the printer wasn't working. Cue ten minutes of faffing to fix the printer. Then my colleague spent another five minutes looking for an envelope to put it in. The whole scenario took close to 20 minutes, when it could have been resolved in less than five if we'd just told him we'd email it to him.

After this interaction, we discussed whether we should start charging €20 if someone wants to collect a physical copy of a reference, while offering to email it to them free of charge as an incentive for them to choose the digital option. Interestingly, since we've applied this €20 charge for anyone who wants a printed reference, everyone who asks is happy with the digital version. That's not to say we don't want to help people, but in this day and age tasks like this add value to no-one.

Chapter 7: Systems and Processes

As the great Warren Buffett once said: "I can buy anything I want, basically, but I can't buy time."[6]

INTERROGATE YOUR PROCESSES

There's no escaping the fact that when you're looking for ways to improve your systems or processes, you need to get into the details. You have to interrogate each and every process in your business to work out if you are doing it in the most efficient way, or if it's a legacy process that needs updating and could be much more efficient. As I said in Chapter 6 when talking about development, it's vital that you question everything to make sure you're not just doing things the way they've always been done, especially if you have a business that's been going as long as ours has!

The whole point of systems and processes is to improve business efficiency, so you need to make sure that they are delivering. Interrogate everything, from how you advertise rental properties

---

6   Lashbrooke, B. (2019) "Warren Buffett Thinks You Cannot Buy Time, But What If You Could?," *Forbes*, 24 January. Available at: https://www.forbes.com/sites/barnabylashbrooke/2019/01/24/warren-buffett-thinks-you-cannot-buy-time-but-what-if-you-could/?sh=7c41b7525fd7.

and conduct viewings to how you collect data and how long it takes from a property becoming vacant for a new tenant to move in.

For example, we have started advertising for new tenants two weeks before the current tenant moves out because we realised it always takes a minimum of one week to find a new tenant due to all the reference checking and paperwork. By starting that process sooner, we can have a tenant on standby, who can move in as soon as the previous tenant moves out and any work that needs to be done has been completed. This might sound really basic, but it's something we weren't doing before – and we wouldn't have realised we could improve our efficiency here if we hadn't interrogated all the steps of that process.

When you start interrogating your processes, it's essential to come back to the idea of starting with the end in mind. Make sure you know what you want to achieve. We want to grow our return for our clients, grow our bottom line and remove inefficiencies within the business. That's our broader goal, but then we have to decide what outcome we want from a specific process.

Chapter 7: Systems and Processes

One thing we have found particularly useful is discussing the current processes with our team because sometimes what you think is happening as the business owner isn't the reality for the people actually following the process. When you identify these kinds of gaps, you have to look at why the current process isn't being followed and then come up with solutions as a team, because that makes it much more likely that people will follow the new process.

It could also be the case that what you think sounds like a great idea won't work in practice because you've got a blind spot, whereas your team will identify that immediately because they are the ones doing these tasks day in, day out. Whatever you decide, it's important that nothing is set in stone. You have to stay agile and be open to making changes as you try new things.

This is all about cultivating that reduce, eliminate, automate mindset and, as I discussed in Chapter 6, embracing change. When everyone has this continuous improvement mindset, it is much easier to make your processes more efficient and to adapt to new technology and systems that arise.

Another goldmine of information for interrogating your processes is your customers. Ask them where their frustrations lie, what their pain points are and what bugs them about doing business with you. When you get into the habit of asking these questions and do so from a position of wanting to improve, you'll be amazed by what you learn and how your business improves as a result.

As a visual person, I find it helps to look at my business from the outside in – literally. I often stand on the opposite side of the street and then walk into the office, imagining what it would be like for me as a customer. Just think about all the mini steps in each of your processes, what needs to be done for that to work and whether it's necessary at all.

During a call, one of our landlords recently highlighted some shortcomings in our maintenance department. It was a brilliant opportunity to receive such valuable insights. Vereshia, our South Africa-based VA, was immediately on a mission to sort out the highlighted issues. When you have a mindset of continuous improvement in your team, nobody takes the feedback as criticism, but instead sees it as an opportunity to improve.

Chapter 7: Systems and Processes

KNOW WHAT GOOD LOOKS LIKE

Interrogating your processes is all well and good, but if you don't have any idea of what good looks like it will be very difficult to make substantial improvements. Our journey of improvement started in earnest when we attended that proptech conference. It opened my mind to the technology that was out there that could help us, and made me think about how the likes of self-service platforms would also be better for our customers.

As I've said, it was spending time in Kristjan's calm, quiet, efficient office that was the real light bulb moment for me. That was when I knew what good looked like, and I'd urge you to find a business you can visit to help you gain clarity over your vision. Once I knew what we were striving for, it was all about implementation and execution.

Being part of mastermind groups is another great way to see what's out there and help you define what good looks like. I continuously learn from what others are doing and can't tell you how much I've learned from my mentors over the years. Continuous learning is the key to business success.

Once you know what good looks like and have your vision for what you want to achieve, you need to help the rest of your team see this too. They have to buy into your vision. You need everyone on your bus to buy into the change, otherwise they will throw up roadblocks and you'll struggle to make the improvements you're aiming for.

When we first started changing our business processes, there were a few people on our bus who struggled with the change and these people are no longer on the bus today. We need everyone to be absolutely committed to positive change and continuous improvement, which is why it's so important to know your values when you're hiring. Although we had objections when we first started moving towards a quieter, calmer office, Maria and I carried out a risk-reward analysis. We knew we didn't want a noisy, clunky business that's expensive in more ways than one.

Everyone in the business now understands that change is part of our culture and they know that this is how we do business – we challenge, we innovate and we always seek to improve. But it wasn't always like that and it's taken time and pain to get to where we are today. How much pain you're prepared to accept to reach your desired outcome is up to you.

Chapter 7: Systems and Processes

I think this process is like going to the gym. It can be very difficult, especially at the beginning. Your motivation can slip for the slightest thing and it can be very painful. However, if you're consistent and continuously lift those weights, it becomes bearable, maybe even fun, and you start to see the changes in your body. It's no different in business.

When you're implementing changes, it can be very easy to feel as though you're going nowhere, but over time you will look back and realise how far you've come. It's transformational when you persevere and keep your end goal in mind. It's massively rewarding to see all that we've achieved, but this process doesn't end! We are always learning about new ways we can improve and so the cycle begins again – although it's much easier now that we have the right people on the bus.

Of course, introducing new pieces of technology costs money, so it's important to carry out a return on investment and cost-benefit analysis of each one. When you free up the time of your team by automating or eliminating some of those boring, repetitive, manual tasks what do you gain? Number one, you give them the capacity to do other value-adding work. Number two, you make your employees' jobs more enjoyable. Number three, in the long term your employee retention will improve (and, therefore, your recruitment costs will decrease) because you have the right people on the bus.

If you're still unsure about whether a piece of technology or another investment is right for your business, come back to that all-important question: *What problem are you trying to solve? What is your end goal?* Begin with the end in mind, because it makes it much easier to identify the worthwhile investments from the shiny tech that might look good, but will add little in terms of real value.

When you take this approach, you will find you make decisions that are based on more than the cost of a solution alone. Take Offr as an example. I know a lot of agencies that don't use it because you have to pay a subscription and you have to pay for each property that you list, but for us it was a no-brainer to start using it. It means we don't have to send out 120 text messages; the system is set up for fantastic communication and the customer experience is through the roof. We've got happier clients, happier buyers, happier sellers and a fully transparent system, all of which ties in with our values.

Often you won't offset the cost of your new technology or tools on day one, but you have to look at them as long-term

Chapter 7: Systems and Processes

investments. This is why it's so important to carry out your cost-benefit analysis, because this will show you the benefits you can realise over the longer term. There may also be some pain when you implement new processes, so make sure you've shown your team what the benefits are and what good looks like so that they are prepared to work through this with you and come out the other side.

Arrange for them to talk to people who have succeeded with whatever it is you're attempting to introduce. I guarantee that when you show them what success looks like, rather than just telling them, you'll have a team that not only accepts change, but is excited by it.

Steps for success

- Know what you want to achieve and why – begin with the end in mind.

- Audit and interrogate your processes – apply the reduce, eliminate, automate mindset and explore how you can add value. Continue to audit and check your processes, and schedule time to check.

- Bring your team with you – show them what good looks like to get buy in for change.

- Take action – create a plan for rolling out new processes and systems, and stick to it.

- Learn from others – find people in the industry who you can consult with, and learn how to do things better from one another.

CHAPTER 8

MIND THE MONEY

I've always known that money and finances are an important part of business, but that doesn't mean I've always been good at managing the money coming into and going out of the business. Like most entrepreneurs, when I started out I was totally clueless about business finances. And like most entrepreneurs, I got "busy" – busy answering phones, busy going to appointments, busy closing deals. I was busy working in the business rather than working on it.

Even back then, I had someone working on our accounts, but the problem was I didn't know what I needed to know. As it turned out, the person running our accounts department was very disorganised – the day I walked into her office to find files everywhere and her looking like a rabbit caught in the headlights, I knew things had to change. Even then, I didn't realise how bad things were, but I did recognise that we had a major lack of systems in our accounting department and that this presented a huge risk to the business.

To help sort out this mess – and this all happened over 14 years ago – I hired a chartered accountant on a consultancy basis. With hindsight, that might have been a bit of overkill, but he did a great job and helped us bring in someone to run our accounts. Ever since then, we've been sharpening the saw and technology has played a huge part in how we've improved our efficiency within our accounting practices.

I know what you're thinking – what if I don't have the resources to pay someone else to do this for me? My view is that you can't afford not to have someone doing it for you. The thing is, if you don't know your numbers inside out, you're flying blind. It's a bit like trying to drive a car at night with no headlights – you won't know where you're going or spot any obstacles coming up on the road ahead.

Chapter 8: Mind the Money

Engaging a very good accountant is important. Do lots of research and ask advice from someone you admire in business. We recently moved accountants and outsourced our accounts. Previously we had done our own profit and loss, inputting of invoices, wages etc, but it's proving much more efficient and cost effective now we've outsourced it.

When you start out in business and you don't have a huge number of transactions going through your books, it can be easy to get away with having a sloppy system in place. But instead of making do, I urge you to shift your mindset and instead focus on investing in the systems, technology and people you will need as you grow. Like anything in life, success comes down to having good habits in place, so if you are just starting out, why not start with good habits? It's far more efficient than starting with bad ones that you have to break! When you put the right systems in place from the beginning, they will be able to grow with your business too, saving you time, and likely money, in the long run.

WHAT CAN YOU STREAMLINE?

One question to ask yourself in relation to the financial management in your business is, "What can I automate?" There is so much incredible technology available these days that can automate a great deal of your accounting systems. We use Xero and by simply having an accounts@ and an invoices@ email address connected to the software, it is able to automatically collect and add invoices into our system. The amount of hours this has saved is incredible. We didn't know about this function until we recently moved to our new accountants.

This is all about finding efficiencies in everything you do. As the saying goes, time is money – so where can you save time and, therefore, make more money? Software like InventoryBase is a good example because it automates a lot of the processes associated with carrying out property inspections. By reducing the amount of time we spend on these low-value activities, we make space for everyone in the team to work on more high-value activities.

High value activities can include marketing activities and making client calls. I mentioned these before and I mention them here again, because it's so important to work on a pipeline

Chapter 8: Mind the Money

of business. The actions we take today are a bit like planting vegetables, we reap what we sow.

Of course, all of these pieces of software and technology cost money, but the key is to view them as a long-term investment rather than as a cost. They might cost you €3,000 to purchase, but how much more business could you bring into your agency if you were spending more time calling clients or carrying out valuations rather than writing up inventory reports? Not only that, but these pieces of software improve the customer experience as well as saving you time – they're a win-win. They also give you a competitive advantage. This is something you can promote when presenting your company for a contract or to a prospective client. If you are only competing on fees then it's likely to be a race to the bottom.

When we hired our new general manager John in 2022, he offered some fantastic suggestions for streamlining our accounting practices, having spent years working in corporate banking. One of his recommendations was to outsource our accounts and by doing so we have reduced our overall expenses by five per cent. This comes back to what I talked about in Chapter 3, about having the right people on your bus. Just as with other areas of your business, you need to make sure you bring smart people onto your team who are always looking for how they can improve your existing processes.

You can also look at your business model itself, rather than just focusing on the accountancy systems you have in place, to see if there is any way to generate regular, recurring income. A lot of estate agents focus on property sales and avoid property management. However, our property management service has been a lifeline because every month all the rent comes into our account, we deduct our fees and then we pay our clients. Our management service works a lot like a subscription service at a gym. Our clients make monthly payments for the work we do, which means we know there will be money coming in every month. It's a recurring revenue model and very important for the overall health of the business.

The difficulty with selling properties is that you don't receive any money until the sale closes. You might have over 20 properties on the market with your business, but if those sales haven't closed yet, you're left waiting for the money to come in after you've spent money on wages, marketing and any other associated costs. Often those sales won't have closed for reasons outside of your control, but that doesn't help you when you need that money to continue trading. It's incredibly

Chapter 8: Mind the Money

stressful if you know you have wages to pay on Friday, but not enough money in the bank to cover them. Looking at a spreadsheet that tells you you'll have €20,000 in fees coming in next month doesn't help one bit if you need that money this Friday.

To help mitigate that risk, we ask for our marketing fees upfront, so that we're not spending money before receiving any payment from our clients. As I've said, we also have our property management services, which means we have cash coming into the business every month. Our property management services include the rental of properties, rent collection, coordination of maintenance, the management of any rent arrears and property inspections.

If you're just starting out in the world of estate agencies, I would strongly recommend that you consider how you can build a recurring revenue model, because it is extraordinarily difficult in business if you're having to wait three, four or five months to be paid for the job you do. Sadly, that's the nature of the property industry, but thinking about this from the start could help you avoid a great deal of stress later in your journey.

It's also important to work out credit terms with your contractors and suppliers. Negotiate good terms and ask your contractors if they can refer any business your way.

Always remember though that cash is king. Regardless of your profit and loss you need to have money in the bank to pay the bills. You need to monitor your sales to ensure that you are getting paid as quickly as possible. In order to do that you have to ensure that each sale is moving through the process as swiftly and efficiently as possible. It's one thing having a big sale with a fee of €8,000, but another if it takes six months to get paid. A monthly cash flow analysis is very important to make sure you have enough money in your bank account to pay expenses every single month. As the business owner, it's essential you are on top of this.

PAY YOURSELF FIRST

I know this might sound controversial to some entrepreneurs and I know many who work in their businesses and either don't get paid or pay themselves very little. However, I urge you to pay yourself first. From the day I set up my business, I made sure this was the case because I didn't have a choice – I needed

Chapter 8: Mind the Money

that money to pay my rent, put fuel in my car and feed myself. I was fortunate that during the early years of the business I didn't have any dependents.

The problem is, if you start out by not paying yourself properly it becomes a habit and you ultimately end up resenting your business and your clients because you're working incredibly hard, but don't have enough money to survive. You have to pay yourself a living wage and you have to prioritise yourself because you deserve to be paid. I'm not saying you'll be in a position to pay yourself a CEO's salary when you're starting out, but you should be able to survive comfortably. Finally, make sure you start a pension as soon as possible. Starting your pension now could help you do the things you've always wanted to do when you retire.

WATCH OUT FOR VANITY ACTIVITIES

Before you take on a particular property or get involved in a new area of business, ask whether this will generate income for your business. In this business it can be easy to get dragged into "vanity listings" – and I've certainly fallen for this in the past – whereby a client wants €100,000 over the guide price, for example, and because it's a beautiful property you take it on because you think it will *look good* to have it on your books.

The thing is, if the property is wildly overpriced you won't sell that home for the price the client wants and you, therefore, won't get paid. It doesn't matter how much work you put into marketing a property if it isn't valued correctly. All that will happen is that you work for free, and more than likely end up with an unhappy client at the end of it. In fact, you would be better to go fishing than waste your time on these vanity listings that go nowhere.

There is great maturity in learning to say no to these kinds of listings – it isn't always easy, but when you do you'll find your time is much better spent because the work you are doing is generating income for the business, rather than sapping your energy for no reward.

Learning to say no, not only to these kinds of property listings, but also to tasks that won't add value to your business in general is really important. As an entrepreneur it is very easy to become a busy fool, and God knows I've been there. These days I am much more ruthless with my time and I have a laser focus on meaningful activity for the business, most of the time anyway.

Chapter 8: Mind the Money

Before you say yes to any activity, ask yourself whether it will deliver a meaningful return on the time you spend doing it. You might be asked to be on a committee, for example, which could be very flattering. But before you accept, just consider whether that committee will help you generate new business and, therefore, whether it's worth your time. Or ask yourself if it is aligned with your future plans and goals.

Another vanity metric within the estate agency industry is having a big office with huge overheads – in this day and age do you really need that? The days of needing a high-profile high street office are gone in my opinion. Could that money be better spent elsewhere, or could you find another way of having a physical premises, such as by sharing an office with another business? Or are there any other resources that you don't need all the time that you could share with another business in your area, whether that's a staff member or a piece of equipment like a printer. Serviced offices are a great option in today's world, and a great way of meeting other people in business – people who could be on your bus, potential clients or advocates.

Don't feel that you need to do things the same way everyone else does – remember Chapter 5, be a challenger. The status quo may not be the best way to approach your business, but if no-one else is doing it, that doesn't mean it's a bad idea. Be your own person and be sensible with your money, especially when you're just starting out. What I've learned over the years is that it's the small things that add up to big results. There are no shortcuts or silver bullets.

You also have to be particularly mindful of your money during the good times, because this is when it's easy to get carried away. Make sure you always have a strong pipeline of business and that you're always sowing the seeds for the next season. Think of this like planting potatoes – if you wait until you're down to your last potato before you start planting new seeds, you'll have no new crops when that last spud is gone. You need to keep planting those seeds, even when you have a big store of potatoes and it's no different in business.

TURNOVER IS VANITY, PROFIT IS REALITY

How many businesses have you seen boasting about record turnover one month and then going bust the next? Having high turnover can sound impressive, but what really counts is

Chapter 8: Mind the Money

the profit you're left with each month, and most importantly the cash in the bank. This is how much money you make after all your expenses. If your turnover is €1 million, but your wage bill and other expenses come in at €900,000, you're only making a profit of €100,000. Meanwhile, there's another estate agency down the road that only has a turnover of €400,000 but that's making a profit of €250,000 – I know which business I'd rather be at the head of.

In the world of property, it can be easy to compare yourself to other agents – being impressed by the number of properties they have listed, or the car they drive, or the size of their office, but always ask yourself, what are their outgoings? Sometimes small is beautiful. When you have a small business it's agile and you can make decisions quickly. I also find that focusing on my own business and staying in my own lane makes me happier.

Also consider what properties you take on. Often it's the lower value homes that sell the fastest, so you get your fees more quickly and the clients are delighted by how quickly the process has moved. In my experience, the really expensive houses can take a long time to sell, so even though it might look impressive that you have those listings, if they aren't bringing you any money then your business will run into trouble.

Having a good mix of properties definitely helps with cash flow. We love having premium homes to sell and they can sell as quickly, and close as efficiently, as the more modestly priced homes – as long as these homes are presented beautifully and our clients have realistic market price expectations. Be careful of sellers who have aspirations that are wildly over market value. They can sit there and take up a lot of time without generating any income. I can think of three big vanity listings we had that chewed up loads and loads of time, but delivered zero revenue.

Whatever type of property business you build, it's important that you don't live hand to mouth and that you make enough money that you're able to build up a cushion for a rainy day. The early days of the business were incredibly tough and I had to get creative and do other activities (like the event organising I mentioned earlier) to generate enough income. The rental properties just weren't there to fully support the business in 1997, but when the apartment blocks were built in 2004, everything changed.

Chapter 8: Mind the Money

STOP THE FREEBIES

Everything adds up in business, just as it does in life. There was never a truer phrase than, "Mind the pennies and the pounds will look after themselves." Make sure you are constantly evaluating everything you're doing, and particularly any activities you do for free. Ask yourself why you offer them free of charge and look at how much time and energy goes into delivering them. Even if you'd only charge €50 for a particular activity, that will add up over the course of 100+ clients.

As the business has evolved, we've become a lot more mindful about the value of our time and, as a result, changed how we operate. For example we used to carry out property inspections free of charge as part of our property management service.

However, with all of the increased legislation and costs of doing business we now charge for a property inspection. We also charge administration fees for various additional services outside of the basic property management package. We have invested heavily in our property management service and the technology, and therefore we can't have an all-inclusive, buffet-style business.

You wouldn't go to your accountant and expect them to throw in a free service – you pay for absolutely everything.

Property management, while great for providing that recurring stream of income, can also be a drain on your resources if it's not managed properly. It is hugely labour intensive and many clients just don't understand everything that goes into it. They are of the view that they pay us ten per cent for the month and for that fee they should receive an all-inclusive buffet. We have found that the clients who expect the all-inclusive buffet are the most demanding, so we have parted ways and we are a better, more profitable and happier business as a result.

My mastermind groups helped me to realise that the estate agency business as an industry gives way too much away for free. Think about your solicitor – you hire them for a job and you pay for the time it takes them to do that job. They don't give away complimentary contracts – they bill for everything based on their time spent on the work.

While we can't bill for time in the same way a solicitor or an accountant might, we have looked at all the elements of our business and have started charging for things that we just used to give away for free, even though they have immense value.

Chapter 8: Mind the Money

As I said, we used to carry out free property inspections twice a year for all the properties we managed. When you add that up over 350 clients, that is a lot of time and resources.

For each client, that doesn't add up to a lot over the month, but for us as a business it makes a huge difference to our overheads. The point is that it's important you look at every service you provide and really interrogate the entire process; exploring what investment you put into delivering it versus what your clients pay for it. When you add up what you spend on technology, staff and time, it can be quite scary. Once you've decided to start charging for something you previously did for free, it's vital that you communicate this well to your clients.

You also have to accept that you might lose some along the way. When we introduced our fees for property inspections some of our clients left, but that's okay because we know we can't continue to provide the level of service they want for the price they're willing to pay. We wish them well and are happy to say goodbye. What we've realised is that it's often the clients who want discounts or who don't want to pay extra that eat up 80 per cent of your time, even though they only provide a very small percent of your income. Time is our most valuable commodity and, therefore, we have to charge for it accordingly. We don't want to be busy fools, so while we will lose some business in the short term through our new approach, we know it will make the business stronger in the long term.

KNOW YOUR PLACE IN THE MARKET

We have also increased our sales fees in the last year because we know we do an excellent job for our clients and provide a lot of added value. In Ireland, agents typically charge fees of between one and two per cent; whereas in the US or Australia agent fees are closer to six per cent. You have to decide where you sit in the market and set your fees accordingly. We know we're not a one per cent agency, so we charge more.

We provide bespoke marketing, beautiful professional photography, 360 degree tours of properties, agent-presented videos, intense social media promotion, a team of three behind marketing, great negotiation skills and first-class customer service. To deliver all of that and then charge bargain basement prices just doesn't make sense. We've accepted that we're not for everyone. It takes bravery to make that decision, but when we look at the value of our services, we know we're worth it and we know that the right clients will see that. We are confident

Chapter 8: Mind the Money

that we offer a service and extras that our competitors don't. It's very important that you know what makes you different when you are negotiating your fees. You need to be able to stand out in a crowded market.

Ultimately, it's not viable as a business to provide the level of service we do and only charge a one per cent fee. We won't be profitable if we do that because of the time and investment we put into everything from our marketing to our processes. Don't forget, it's not about having the most listings if you want to be successful in business – it's about being profitable, making money and enjoying the journey. I know an amazing estate agent in the UK and he only sells a handful of properties at a time. Mind you, they are very high-end homes, but he offers a really bespoke service and charges much higher fees than his competitors as a result.

KEEP LEARNING

Put time in your diary every month to analyse your figures – remember what gets scheduled and measured gets done. You have to go into your accounts department and get under the bonnet of your processes to see where you can improve efficiencies, and what technology might be available to streamline or automate some of your processes. Keep asking if there's a way of working smarter, faster or better.

If business finance is something you particularly struggle with, who can you go to for help? Could you find a mentor through an enterprise board or business organisation? Check your local Chambers of Commerce for training opportunities. In the UK you could join Agents Together, which is a not for profit that provides free personal and professional mentoring to estate agents. Join forums for business leaders as well as those in the estate agency sector.

Surround yourself with people who know more than you so that you are always learning. This is how you grow. You can learn a lot just by reading books, watching videos and listening to podcasts from other people who have found success in this industry—however you like to learn, the key is to make it part of your routine. Learning is a habit, just like anything else, so carve out time every week to learn more not only about business finance, but about any other areas where you need support. I recently started listening to *Diary of a CEO* with Steven Bartlett. This really sets me up for the day.

Chapter 8: Mind the Money

Often when you learn about how to improve efficiency in other areas of your business it will have a positive impact on your finances. This is how you'll grow your business and achieve even greater success. Remember that while the big deals can be exciting, it's the small, consistent deals that bring the money in each month. Don't neglect those to chase the shiny expensive properties that will make your agency look good. All too often in business, it's the bread and butter listings that are hugely important.

You need to build good habits around your organisation, not just around your business finances, to achieve the efficiencies that will help your business grow. Habit forming isn't sexy – it's about those small, daily tasks that set you up for success. Even if business finance isn't something you want to learn about, you have to make it part of your repertoire as a business owner; you can't afford to neglect it. But I promise that if you build time into your days, and weeks, to learn and grow in this area, eventually it will start to come more naturally and you will reap the rewards.

Steps for success

- Think about cash flow – is there a way for you to generate monthly recurring revenue within your business model? Start saving from day one to give yourself a buffer.

- Know your value – evaluate your services so that you know their (and your) value. Stop giving away freebies and instead charge what you're worth.

- Focus on profit – turnover often sounds impressive, but it's profit that will keep you in business, so look to trim expenses wherever you can.

- Keep learning – don't sit still. Look out for new pieces of technology that can streamline your processes and keep looking for ways to improve.

- Know your numbers – make sure you analyse your accounts every single month. I'm astonished by the number of people in business who don't know their numbers. What's your profit margin, how much cash is in the bank, what are your revenue streams, any areas for savings and so on, are the questions you need to answer.

CHAPTER 9

TRAIN HARD

When I talk about training, I also mean learning in whatever form that takes, whether it's from books, courses, podcasts, mentors, other people in the business or your network. You also learn from mistakes – and when you have a good network of people and team around you, you can learn from their mistakes too.

Self-development and continuous improvement are essential to achieve success. If you don't continue to train and upskill, you can lose your edge. Imagine if you woke up tomorrow with a six-pack and fully toned body, but had no idea how to train to keep it. Unless you very quickly learned how to train, how to eat and how to manage your health, you would likely be back to where you started within weeks or months simply because you didn't know what you had to do to maintain that physique. Business is no different. If you haven't had to train to achieve business success and made some mistakes along the way, you won't know what you need to do to maintain it.

It's easy to get complacent about your continuous improvement – whether that's training or learning. Running an estate agency is very time consuming and we are all busy in the doing and the now. Training and personal development is the "important and not urgent" stuff, so it can get neglected, but if we only focus on the "urgent" stuff we don't set ourselves up for success. Here's a snapshot of the type of learning my team and I love to do:

» Completing online and in person training through the Institute of Professional Auctioneers and Valuers (IPAV) and gaining CPD hours
» Attending the Sanjfest estate agency conference London or online
» Being part of Sanjay's mastermind group
» Being part of Jerry Lyons' estate agents honesty group

Chapter 9: Train Hard

- » Going to in-person Waterford Chamber Leadership events with expert speakers
- » Attending regular training courses run by the local enterprise office (LEO)
- » Participating in training courses run by the Waterford-based marketing company Márla Communications
- » Listening to industry podcasts which I detailed earlier
- » E-learning through online platforms, particularly management and leadership training
- » Attending the various training events online and in-person that John Paul runs in the UK
- » Working with Stephen Brown, a UK estate agency training coach
- » Working with regular trainers who do in-person strategy sessions with me and the team
- » Working with a couple of different mentors at a time
- » Having a wellness coach who has run four team events over six months in 2023
- » In-house training through role play, this happens a lot on the job
- » Trainuel employee training software is updated regularly and the team have to continuously upskill

THERE ARE NO INSTANT RESULTS

I've always loved exercising and I trained consistently at the gym for over 20 years, until around 2020/21. During this time, I had to undergo a big operation and I developed long Covid after catching Covid-19 three times. Being unable to train because of my health had an impact not only on my physical health, but also on my mental health and self-esteem. It wasn't what I was used to and I missed exercising.

In January 2023, I felt well enough to go back to the gym and I decided I would build up to going three times per week, no matter what. The first few weeks were incredibly hard and I was only going to the gym twice a week – I had to start some-where. But I felt so weak; all my strength had gone and I was struggling to lift anything. I remember the first day I went back to the gym I got really upset. I looked in the mirror and cried, thinking, *Oh my God, how did I put on so much weight and lose all my muscle?*

I knew I couldn't go on like this, but I also know it takes time to change your body and I couldn't expect instant results. One thing I could change immediately though was my attitude, so I adopted an attitude of gratitude.

Chapter 9: Train Hard

Instead of comparing myself to the body I had three years ago, I compared myself to where I was 12 months before, when I felt so crap I couldn't even get to the gym. Now I looked in the mirror and thought, *Isn't it fantastic that my body brought me here today?* I cried again, but this time I felt happy. I kept telling myself, *Isn't it great that I'm here? I'm grateful to be back at the gym. I'm going to cultivate this attitude of gratitude and I'm going to hold myself accountable for coming here three times every week.*

Since then, I've not only been going to the gym regularly each week, but I've also hired a personal trainer because I decided that in 2023 my health was going to be my biggest focus. I'm the pilot of my plane in both my family and my business, and if I can't fly that plane then it crashes.

By April of 2023, I was going to the gym three times per week and walking another three days – the difference I noticed in my abilities was extraordinary. It reminds me of the difference I've seen in our business in the few years leading up to me writing this book – each time we've brought in a new piece of technology or a new, high-calibre member of the team or mentor, it's taken time before we've seen the full impact.

When our new manager joined, I told him it would take six months before he'd really know what he was doing and be in a position to add real value to the business. To get to a point where you can add value, you have to train, just like you do at the gym if you want to gain strength or lose weight. John committed to all the training and coaching we provided in his first six months and then he was flying; just like I saw a significant improvement in my strength by committing to training at the gym, two then three times a week, along with the extra walking I was doing.

My attitude of gratitude has paid off — when I look at myself now, and compare myself to how I was in January 2023, I'm delighted. I don't think about where I was three years ago and I certainly don't compare myself to other people — comparing yourself to others is the enemy in business, you have to look at how far you've come rather than at what other people are doing.

If I'd compared myself to people I consider to be "rockstar agents" I would never have written this book. There are people in the estate agency business who have way more profitable, successful businesses than me. I asked myself a lot of questions before I started this process, *Am I really going to write this book? Am I worthy of writing this book?* But what I realised is that

Chapter 9: Train Hard

our view of success is subjective and I have a lot to share, and I've had a lot of success. I really hope that if you are reading this book there will be a couple of things you take away and implement – if it helps you, then my book is a success.

When I hear people I consider to be successful defining success on their terms, it's rarely about business profits. More often than not success is being healthy, or having adult children who want to spend time with you, or being happy. My advice is not to compare yourself to anyone else, but to instead focus on what success looks like for you. You have to train hard and put the work in, but in the end the race is only with yourself. While you are at it, don't forget to boost your wellbeing and build in time for you to relax and de-stress. It's very important (look back at the tips I shared in Chapter 6).

MAKE A PLAN – AND STICK TO IT

As I've said many times throughout this book, you have to begin with the end in mind. Ask yourself what you want to achieve, and give an answer that doesn't involve comparing yourself with others. I can't stress how important it is to have clarity over what you want to achieve – without knowing that end goal you're like a bull in a china shop.

When I went back to the gym, I wanted to gain muscle, tone up and lose weight – I wanted to feel fantastic and I knew what that looked like for me. When I started transforming the business, I knew what I wanted it to look like because I'd seen how Kristjan and his team at Base worked. I wanted to introduce that same level of efficiency and calm to Liberty Blue. We are achieving all of these goals because we are being consistent.

Too many people start working towards a goal, but give up long before they achieve it because they want everything to happen overnight. They want to see instant results, but life just isn't like that. There is no silver bullet – you are only going to get results if you are consistently putting in the work to get you closer to your goals.

Our Live After 5s, where we jump on our social media channels to share a short, live video every day, are a good example. I only started doing these regularly because Sanjay, who runs one of my mastermind groups, challenged us to give it a go and promised a prize – a coaching session with Lisa Novak, a top

Chapter 9: Train Hard

estate agent in Australia, who I love and admire – for anyone who was consistent.

Never one to turn down a challenge and desperate to win that coaching session, I started recording a Live After 5 every day, Monday to Friday. I won. Two and a half years later, we are still going and everyone in our area knows about our Live After 5s. Right now I'm pleased to say we have introduced two other team members to doing the Lives. In fact, Vereshia is now doing live videos all the way from South Africa to our audience mainly based in Ireland. When you have the right people on the bus anything is possible.

Lisa even told me during our session that I should keep doing our Live After 5s and assured me that one day clients would turn up after having been watching the content for ages and want to commit to our business because they know and trust us. She was right. While I was writing this book, we had a new client sign up with us to rent and manage her property after having watched our Live After 5s for the past couple of years.

Imagine if we'd given up after just a few weeks of producing those videos – we'd never have built the audience we have or reached people like our new client. Because we've consistently

237

shown up as helpful experts, people have come to know, like and trust us, and our business by association. All of this connects back to our mission as well: we want to be known as helpful experts and champions of Waterford because it's a great place to live.

But we don't just turn up every day without knowing what we're going to talk about. We have a weekly communications plan, which includes topics that speak to the various audiences we want to help. So, on Monday our Live After 5 might be targeted to landlords, then on Tuesday it will share something helpful for tenants. On Wednesday we might be talking to buyers and on Thursday investors. Friday might be more fluid, where we choose a story of the day. Having a plan helps me and the rest of the team to show up consistently as helpful experts, because we can prepare what we're going to say and there are no excuses for not jumping on camera. That said, some weeks we haven't gotten around to creating a plan so we just go down the road of helpful tips. It's absolutely fine to repeat topics which have been discussed before.

These Live After 5s aren't perfect – we have bloopers and we make mistakes – but that just shows our audience our vulnerabilities. It's raw and it's real. People are getting to know us

Chapter 9: Train Hard

and we know that we're not for everyone, that's fine – if we're not the right fit for someone, we wish them well. But we also know that the right people will find us, see what we're about and they'll show up.

Having a plan is important, but without action a plan won't get you anywhere – a training plan won't give you six-pack abs, but going to the gym three (or more) times a week and following that plan likely will. You need to know how you're going to implement what you've learned. For example, if someone goes on a course, they have to report back to the whole team about what they've learned and how they're going to convert that into action. Training hard doesn't mean that your training has to be hard work. It refers to the fact that your training needs to be consistent, and for many of us that is often the hardest part to master.

LEARN TO SAY "NO"

It can be very easy to take on more and more, especially when you're running and building a business, but time is our most precious commodity and we have to be very careful what we say yes to. I know that I worked hard during the Covid-19 pandemic and that led to burnout. You have to leave some juice in the tank, otherwise you're no use to anyone. You also need to encourage your staff to do the same.

A colleague recently had a Friday off and, as he was getting ready to leave the office on Thursday, I asked what he was planning to do over the weekend. "I'm going to a business networking event at 7.30am tomorrow, that'll be finished at 9.30am, and then I'll be off for the rest of the weekend."

"Why are you going to that event?" I asked.

"I feel guilty because I've missed the last couple," he replied.

"Why are you worrying about that? You've been too busy. Why would you go to that event tomorrow? It isn't a high priority, save your energy, invest in yourself and come back on Monday feeling refreshed," I told him. He took my advice, had a relaxing long weekend and felt better the following week for having given himself that time off.

Encouraging your team to take breaks is one thing, but it's important to lead by example and carve out time for ourselves as leaders too – and also to ensure we're not overcommitting. For

Chapter 9: Train Hard

example, I'm a board member at our Chamber of Commerce and in 2023 I was asked if I'd join the board of another professional body. In the past, I'd have thought *Regina, isn't that absolutely fabulous to be asked to do that! Say yes!* That would be my ego talking.

However, this time I politely said no to the opportunity because I knew it would be a distraction and that it's not aligned with my mission and vision. I also know my own personality is full duck or no dinner – once I commit to something I put the work in, but I knew that if I put the work into this other organisation, I wouldn't have enough energy and time to dedicate to the plan for my business.

I'm still a board member for our local Chamber of Commerce though because I enjoy it, want to give back to the community and it aligns with my broader business mission. I've also realised that when you say yes to one thing, you are saying no to something else. We can't do everything – and that "something else" might be quality time with your family. The lessons are to put the work in, but make sure it's going into the right places, and to be very careful what you say yes to.

Look at anyone who's considered successful and you'll realise they are very ruthless with their time. Our estate agency coach John Paul won't go to any meeting unless it has an agenda and a schedule. His view is that if a meeting isn't organised, it won't be worthwhile, and he's right. You have to protect your energy and your time to ensure you have the energy you need to dedicate to achieving your goals.

Because time is such a precious commodity, you also have to find ways to be as efficient as possible with your time. Of course, the first time you do anything it will take you longer than the 20th time, so practice and repeat is a useful mantra. But there are other ways you can use your time more efficiently. As you know by now, video content is an important part of how we promote Liberty Blue, but creating it can be time consuming, so we often batch record our videos.

For example, we recorded five videos for a new homes development in one afternoon. We had a plan of the tips we wanted to run through in each video, and the final one would be a walk through of the house. I took different jackets and outfits so I could change between each video, and we shot each one in a different location in the development. By the end of the day we had five videos that we could share over the course of the next

Chapter 9: Train Hard

five weeks. By batching those videos, we saved hours of time and created great content on a day when I was in the zone.

YOU ALWAYS NEED TO BE TRAINING

Training isn't only for you as the business owner, it's also for the people on your team. When it comes to training for your staff, the onboarding process is obviously very important. You need a plan for each new person coming in and they will have to train hard for those first few weeks, but then both you and they reap the benefits.

However, it's just as important that the training doesn't stop at the onboarding. Once you have trained people in your business, and they understand their role within it and how the company works, you have to continue to develop their skills, offer further training and help them to evolve and improve alongside the business. You're only as strong as your weakest link, which is why it's so important to have the right people on the bus and make sure that once they're there, they are constantly developing their skills. Think back to the concept of investing in your people, which I discussed in Chapter 6.

This training doesn't have to be in the form of a course – for example, our manager meets with each member of the team for a one-to-one bi-weekly. These are an opportunity to assess how the week has gone and for the manager to do any coaching that's needed. This allows people to adjust and correct behaviours that may need to change as they go and usually before they turn into bigger issues. During these one-to-ones they will also identify any skill gaps, review each person's KPIs and ask what each person has learnt that week. Making upskilling part of these one-to-one conversations instils a culture of continuous learning.

Our daily staff meetings also fall under training hard, because they are a consistent touchpoint for each person in the business, and a chance to ask questions or raise concerns. The key is to keep all of these aspects of your training consistent.

In addition, I also run coaching sessions with anyone on the team who needs additional support with specific skills. Usually these sessions involve role playing because I've found this is a great way to build up someone's confidence in dealing with a potentially difficult conversation and they are a great chance for that person to try different approaches and evaluate what does and doesn't work before they try it "for real". These small

Chapter 9: Train Hard

coaching sessions can be really impactful and I find it's much easier to find time for half an hour, or an hour, here and there with different people than it is to carve out full days to dedicate to "training".

As an example, Vereshia, who's based in South Africa, has just started doing our Facebook Live after 5s. I did some coaching with her and she is brilliant at it. So, now we have an additional member of the team talking to our audiences and giving maintenance advice and tips for the home. There are so many benefits and Vereshia is delighted because it's pushing her outside her comfort zone, and she wants to continuously improve and be challenged. We've introduced a specific live aimed at our landlord audience so that's good for business. It also reduces the pressure for Maria, Darragh and myself as there is another team member onboard.

You also need a comprehensive online training manual that documents every process and system in your business. Think of this like your business operations manual – if you don't have one, you need to write one. Even once you've created this manual, you have to continuously update it. Each time you improve a process, it needs to be documented.

Every single business process, no matter how basic, has to be in there — I'm talking about everything from how you answer the phone to the sales process from start to finish. Don't forget about things like your HR processes and practices for holding one-to-ones either. Your manual also needs to include your mission, values, brand personality — it is the roadmap for your business. We use Trainual and it's brilliant. My good friend Anton, from Sanjay's mastermind group, recommended it — recommendations like this are the benefit of being part of such an amazing group of people who want to share information with you and see you and your business succeed and flourish.

It can be very easy to tell yourself that you're too busy for training, but the problem with this attitude is that you're seeking instant gratification. If you want to be successful in business, you have to take a long-term view and commit to training courses, even if you won't see the benefits from attending them until months down the line. When you put the day-to-day ahead of your long-term goals, you're stuck in the "urgent" stuff in the business and you're letting the "important, but not urgent" stuff build up until it becomes "urgent" which increases the risk of things going wrong or you making a poor decision because you're under pressure.

Chapter 9: Train Hard

As a business owner, you have to do all you can to future-proof and stay ahead of the curve. We all know that things outside of our control can happen and completely change the marketplace – look at how the Covid-19 pandemic affected estate agencies the property market and has changed the way we do business.

What might future-proofing look like? In 2017, Maria and I did a valuation course in Dublin because we had started selling property and were managing a large portfolio. We wanted to improve our competence and learn about best practice. It was a huge investment for both of us to travel to Dublin, particularly in terms of our time and our energy, but it has paid off. What we learned in that course has served us incredibly well and protected us from potential litigation, because it taught us the skills we needed to ensure we did everything right and by the book. Without that knowledge it would have been easy to make mistakes that could have got the business into a lot of trouble.

We are also incredibly fortunate that we moved into sales when we did, because a lot of landlords have left the market in recent years and we would have really struggled if we were still solely reliant on rental management. You always have to

247

look ahead and trust the process of training, even if it feels like a cost in the now, it is an investment in your future.

TRAINING IS FOR LIFE

Training hard is a lifelong commitment. You need to be passionate about your business, otherwise you won't engage with the slightly more boring, less sexy aspects of the training you need to do. I don't think anyone would argue that compliance is sexy, but you need to know it if you're going to run a business in the world of property.

There will also be elements that you really don't enjoy, or that you find particularly difficult, but you have to push through the pain to see the benefits, maintain the success you've achieved so far, and see even more success in the future. It won't all be a beautiful journey of continuous improvement; sometimes it will be a hard slog where you'll feel like you're going backwards, but you have to trust the process.

When you're training with the right people, you know what you're trying to achieve and you have a plan to get you there, it is much easier to go the distance. When you have a passion

Chapter 9: Train Hard

for what you're doing and you're committed to continuous improvement you're happy to put in the work, to sharpen the saw, so to speak.

Training hard means constantly pushing yourself out of your comfort zone – it's the same as increasing the amount you lift in the gym. You gradually build up your weights, but you don't stop adding on. Once you feel confident at 30kg you add a couple more kilos and go from there. Before you know it, you'll be lifting 45kg. Trust that weeks, months or even years from now, you'll look back at what your best was then and realise you've exceeded it.

As the business owner, it's important that you don't just leave training to your team. You need to keep putting yourself out there and expanding your knowledge. When you want to move into new areas, you need to know what good looks like, otherwise how are you going to communicate that to the rest of the team?

WHO'S ON YOUR TEAM?

To build a high-performing business you need a high-performing team. For those people to perform at their best, they need a goal to work towards, a training plan to help them develop and coaching along the way to help them implement what they learn. Think of a football team that wants to win the league. It's not enough to just focus on winning the next match, they need a plan to ensure they're in the best shape to win as many matches as possible throughout the season.

Having high-performing players in the right positions is only the start. If you want to win as many matches as possible, and therefore the league, your players need to train. They need their nutrition to be right; the team needs to have a strong bond and they need a plan of attack for each match. You need all of this for your team too – you have to not only find the best possible players for your team, but you have to help them stay in top shape so they can deliver for your business.

Set expectations for your team and show them that you're committed to them and their development. Our team particularly loves the daily morning meetings – after just a few months of hosting them the feedback was universally positive. It's a

Chapter 9: Train Hard

great way to encourage consistent communication between everyone, which builds trust and rapport in the team. This means that when someone is struggling or not performing at their best, their peers are more likely to step in and ask what they can do to help.

It's also important to consider offering training around wellbeing and mental health, because the happier and more engaged your staff are, the more valued they feel and the harder they'll train.

SET YOURSELF UP FOR SUCCESS

As I said at the start of this chapter, it's important to take care of yourself as the business owner. In addition to looking after your health, you have to ensure you don't forget about your own development and training while you're training others. As I've said throughout this book, one of the keys to setting yourself up for success is to have a mentor.

I wouldn't be without a mentor and I believe every successful person has at least one. If you don't already have one, I urge you to find one. If you're concerned about paying for a professional mentoring programme, consider other options – do you know someone who's retired who may want to share their experience with you and give back? Or is there a mentoring scheme through your local enterprise office or Chamber of Commerce that you could join?

Over the years I have had various mentors, some of them paid, some of them through an enterprise scheme, and three in particular have revolutionised my business. These days your mentors don't even need to be based locally – they can be anywhere in the world. As soon as you start looking for a mentor, you will see potential opportunities everywhere. Just as with any other training, when you start working with a mentor, set out what you want to achieve – begin with the end in mind.

Create a plan together. I can't tell you what your plan will look like, because we each have different goals and ambitions, but when you know your ultimate goal you can work backwards and your plan will fall into place.

I know that when I engaged our business mentor Tony I had a list of goals that I wanted to achieve. Looking at where we have come in the two years we've worked together, it's a different environment and so much better. As I've mentioned, Tony has

Chapter 9: Train Hard

also been coaching John and helped him with his leadership skills, as well as with operational issues when needed. That time and structure would be very difficult for me to commit to and so it's actually worked out brilliantly. So many times in the past, new people joined and after a few days of training were left to get on with it. How can people really thrive in our businesses if we don't invest in them properly and regularly?

Commit to the relationship and commit to spending time each week or month with your mentor. The reason mentoring has such a big impact on a business, and can accelerate your success, is that working with a mentor presents an opportunity to regularly extract yourself from the day-to-day of your business and instead focus on your long-term goals that can be two, three, five or even ten years away. When you can take the time to look to the future, it's much easier to find clarity about the goals of the business and what training and people development is needed to take us from good to great.

Steps for success

- Create a training plan – set goals for the business and align your people development and training with these goals. For example, if you want to grow residential sales, how many licenced estate agents are already in your business and do you need to hire another one or train an existing member of the team to become an estate agent? All this requires planning.

- Focus on continuous learning – make learning and training part of your regular meetings and one-to-ones. Make sure you have a skills matrix and that your team is multi-skilled.

- Learn to say no – protect your time and energy so your focus is in the right place.

- Find mentors – accelerate your progress by training with and learning from others who have been on this journey before. Join a mastermind group so you can share valuable information and support.

- If you want to increase sales and improve your team's selling skills, engage a coach.

CHAPTER 10

DEALING WITH BULLIES AND HATERS

No matter what kind of business you own and run, you'll encounter bullies and haters. They might come in the form of an overly demanding client, or someone threatening you with legal action. Or they might be online trolls who seem to take pleasure in writing nasty things about you and your business. They could even be people who talk about you unfavourably behind your back. Whoever they are, it's important not to let them intimidate you or force you into changing course.

In my 26-plus years in business I've learned the hard way the importance of setting boundaries with clients, particularly in the early stages of a relationship. I will hold my hands up and admit that in the early days of the business, I tolerated bad behaviour and clients who weren't aligned with our values. Now I would just show these people the door. But I understand how easy it is to say yes when you should say no when you're just starting out and really need the money.

I definitely felt as though I had to take a lot of crap from certain bigger clients in my early days. These people weren't aligned with my values or those of the business, and working with them caused me a great deal of internal strife. Externally, I might have shown a lot of confidence, but internally I was anything but. Over the years, I've realised that one of my internal flaws is that I want approval and want to be liked – I'm sure you can relate to this too. It has taken time for me to be comfortable saying no and firing clients, but trust me when I say keeping these kinds of demanding people around is a false economy, no matter how much they're paying you.

TESTING TIMES

Years ago, we took on our first luxury home for sale. The seller was an incredibly demanding man and my mistake was not

Chapter 10: Dealing with Bullies and Haters

setting out my stall and putting boundaries in place from day one. His property was beautiful, but selling it was incredibly stressful. He wanted a concierge service and made absolutely outrageous demands that, with hindsight, I should have refused. But, being new to selling luxury homes, I gave in to what he was asking.

For example, his home was 15 miles from our office but he expected us to hand deliver the contract to him. Then he would ask for irrelevant changes, like a different font on a document, and I'd agree. Looking back, I think he was testing us, but what he was asking was absolutely outrageous. My mistake was being compliant with his requests.

In short, I tolerated his incredibly bad behaviour and highly unreasonable requests from the get-go, and that framed our relationship. When we reached the offer stage on the sale of his house, we didn't get the price he wanted. That's when he switched from being overly demanding to being outright nasty and threatening.

I internalised the whole situation and became incredibly stressed. But I learned some valuable lessons from this experience, the first being how important it is to have good people around you and a network of people who can provide you with professional advice. In this case, I rang the Institute of Auctioneers and Valuers and spoke to the CEO Pat Davitt, who gave me really excellent advice and helped me see that I didn't have to keep working with him, so I fired him. Although I was scared about having that conversation, I felt a huge sense of relief the moment I did – an enormous weight lifted off my shoulders.

Then he became really nasty and started threatening legal action. Again, I turned to my network and took legal advice. They assured me that he was just huffing and puffing – he was a bully making threats in the hope of breaking me down, he had no legal standing. When he realised he wasn't going to get anywhere with his threats, he backed down.

The second lesson I learned from this situation is the importance of setting clear boundaries and turning clients away if you feel they are a bad fit or show any signs of being unreasonable. No matter how much you want to do a good job or sell a property, it will never work out well if your values aren't aligned with those of your client. In fact, the worst thing you can do is work with people who zap your energy, because we need our energy not only for our business, but also for our family,

Chapter 10: Dealing with Bullies and Haters

our team and to live well. If you work with clients who steal all your energy and break you down, you've got nothing left for anybody else.

These days, I firmly believe that protecting my energy, and that of my team, takes precedence over any sum of money. You have to make sure you don't give away your power by being overly compliant, like I was in the past, and set clear boundaries with anyone you decide to work with. Also don't feel as though you have to do business with someone – if you see red flags in their behaviour, just say no and walk away. Thankfully, I can now see who these people are from the get-go, so we don't work with them. I've learnt that we are not for everyone and that feels very empowering.

No matter how much money you need to make or how desperate you are, don't allow people to behave very badly towards you, because this will knock your confidence and stop you from doing great things. It's easy to think that the €5,000, €10,000 or even €20,000 is really important for you to survive in business, but trust me when I say that money isn't worth it if it's coming from someone who treats you badly, saps all your energy and prevents you from moving forwards as a result.

WHAT'S THE WORST THAT WILL HAPPEN?

Having dealt with a number of bullies throughout my career, I've learned that underneath all the bravado they are just chickens. One of the best ways I've found for diffusing these situations, and remaining calm in myself, is to ask, what's the worst that will happen? It's amazing how well this works, even in the face of someone who's full of rage…

Going nuclear

Some years ago, one of the biggest bullies in town wanted us to take on a large maintenance contract for a development. One of my colleagues made a misjudged comment to someone in his organisation and this bully exploded. My colleague apologised for the comment, but he was having none of it. He tried to use it to blackmail us into taking out the contract with him. We weren't going to give him the contract, but agreed we'd meet to discuss it.

Before the meeting, I spoke to my solicitor who advised us to simply apologise, but not expand further. My colleague and

Chapter 10: Dealing with Bullies and Haters

I role played the meeting ahead of time too, and we were expecting fireworks. Sure enough, when the meeting came around, this bully banged his fists on the table and shouted, "I'm going to press the nuclear button if you don't sign up for this contract!"

I jumped up out of my seat. Very calmly, I said, "Can I ask you, are our lives in danger?" He looked shocked. "Are our lives in danger?" I repeated. "Are we safe?"

All the rage and anger dissipated from his face. "Absolutely, there's no danger here," he almost stammered.

"OK, so we are safe. Now, the only other thing in terms of pushing the nuclear button is that you're talking about litigation," I continued. "I'm sorry you feel that way if that's what you want to do. After all, it's a small City and we all do business together. But if you feel that's what you have to do here are my solicitor's details, along with his phone number for your convenience."

I slid a card with my solicitor's address and phone number across the table to him and sat down. I have never seen such a dark cloud turn into a puff of smoke so quickly. All of a sudden he was a different person and started backpedalling.

> "That's not what I meant. Everything is fine..." Shortly after, we all shook hands, the meeting ended and that was the end of it.

When someone threatens you, I find it really useful to start with that question: What's the worst that could happen here? Work backwards from the worst outcome – your life being in danger – until you arrive at the most likely worst outcome from the situation. In the example I just shared, I established our lives weren't in danger. The next danger would be to the business via litigation, but he quickly backed down when I confronted him with this option. From there, it usually becomes a problem that is easy to solve.

Don't get me wrong, doing this in a meeting where someone is banging their fists on the table and being dramatic isn't easy. If someone had behaved like that with me ten years ago, I probably would have vomited on the carpet! But now I've got a simple tool to help me see the situation for what it really is.

So, work through those outcomes. Start with the risk to life – Am I safe? Are my colleagues and my team safe? Are our customers safe? Is anyone going to die?

Chapter 10: Dealing with Bullies and Haters

Then move onto money – Are we going to lose all our money at the touch of a button? Can they sue us? If they do, have we got insurance to cover that? Think about what is within your control and break the situation down. If you know that the person who's shouting at you can't take your money or sue you, they can knock themselves out.

Or, perhaps this is the point at which you ask can we fix this? Can we appease the situation and do we want to? Running through these questions has served me incredibly well over the years and helped me remain calm even in very stressful situations.

STANDING UP TO THE BULLIES

One of my most terrifying experiences of standing up to a bully happened about 14 years ago, around the time of the big property and financial crash in 2008/09. A big client with 50 properties wanted us to transfer his tenants' deposits into his account, rather than keeping the money in our account. Some of the banks were going belly up and he was panicking.

I was not about to transfer the tenants' deposits to him — I knew if that money left our account, we'd never get it back and more importantly, our tenants would never get their money back. But he wasn't budging. My cousin, who has a very senior role in a huge company, told me that if you're in a situation like this, you have to meet face-to-face and eyeball the bully.

So, I drove to Galway with my one-month old baby son and my mother to meet this client. My mother was with my son in a hotel while I went for the meeting. I arrived at the meeting alone to find he'd brought four business associates with him — one woman, to five big men. He was incredibly threatening and kept insisting he wanted the money transferred to his account.

I'd taken legal advice ahead of the meeting, so my Plan B was to suggest that we transfer the tenants' deposit money into a solicitor's escrow account. But he wasn't having any of it. He got really angry, stood up and shouted, "I want my fucking money!"

Firstly, it wasn't his money. But I remember feeling a physical jolt of pain shoot up my back while I was sitting in front of a very large window, with four other men and my client shouting at me — I was terrified that he was going to push me through

Chapter 10: Dealing with Bullies and Haters

the window behind me. I nearly vomited with fear, but then something came over me. I stood up, with tears in my eyes, looked straight at him and said, "You're very brave aren't you? It took you to have four other men in the room to tackle me, a woman who's travelled here on her own, with her mother and one-month-old baby who are in the hotel across the way. Who's really the brave person here? Now sit down and behave yourself!"

He stopped in his tracks. I continued, "How dare you attack me like this, when there's all of you 'big, brave men' here and I'm all on my own. You're threatening me and what you're asking is completely unreasonable." I turned to one of the men he'd brought with him.

"You're a car dealer – if I bought a car from you and then had a problem with it, you wouldn't send me to the manufacturer in Japan to fix it would you? You'd have to sort it. This is no different. The tenants rent the property from us and if there's a problem and they want their money back, they're going to come to us, not to you (the owner). I have to have their money for them."

I could feel my heart pounding in my chest, but as I finished speaking and looked around the room, I could see that what I'd said had landed. The atmosphere completely changed. The client realised he'd overstepped the mark and dialled it right back. His buddies also realised that this was not a good situation.

The conversation went from him demanding money that wasn't his, to the whole group looking for solutions. In the end, I never did transfer the tenants' deposit money, it stayed in our client account. I had stood my ground, stood up to this bully, and got the outcome I needed, that my business needed and that our tenants needed.

CHANGE THE CHANNEL HONEY!

Of course, in this day and age it's not only physical bullies we have to stand up to, but those who attack us online as well. I put myself out there on social media, through our Live After 5s and other content, and luckily it's been rare that I've felt attacked online.

But there will always be people who criticise what you're doing, maybe even laugh at you, sometimes they'll do both those

Chapter 10: Dealing with Bullies and Haters

things only to start copying you! As I said earlier, Lisa Novak (my hero) responds to critics like this by saying, "Why don't you change the channel honey?" If you don't like what I'm putting out on social media, you don't have to watch me. That's my channel and if I'm not for you, that's fine. Change the channel and watch somebody else.

The key is not to let these people derail what you're doing. Not everyone will love what they see, but remember they aren't the people you want to work with anyway. One event that illustrates this really well always sticks in my mind. We were getting quotes for a new sign for our office and one of the people who came to measure up and give us a quote started a conversation with me. He said, "Regina, why are you always on LinkedIn doing videos and posts?"

"It's great for us to get our message out there and talk to people."

"People are sick of seeing you, they all know who you are."

I was quite offended by his comment — needless to say he wasn't going to get my business to make our new sign — but his comment also sparked the doubting Thomases in my head.

267

Maybe he's right? Why am I always doing this? Should I post fewer videos...

As my mind was going round in circles with these self-doubting thoughts, the phone rang. I answered and introduced myself. The lovely man on the other end of the phone said, "Regina, I know who you are, I see you on LinkedIn all the time and I love what you're doing! The reason I'm calling is because a family member has recently passed away and we need to get their house valued for probate – I can't think of anyone we'd love to help us more than you."

Just like that, all those doubting voices in my head vanished. We sold this gentleman's house and he's been a raving fan ever since. But perhaps more importantly, I realised that the guy outside the office measuring for the sign wasn't in our tribe. He wasn't interested in the advice or help I offered via my videos and he wasn't going to become a client, but the gentleman with the house to sell was. Sticking to our brand mission, and our conviction that being helpful experts is the right thing to do, means we're not the right fit for everybody, but that's fine by me.

Chapter 10: Dealing with Bullies and Haters

Knowing who your tribe is really helps you deal with the critics and the haters of the world. It's also important to remember who you're doing things for, because more often than not, the people who throw stones aren't the ones you are working for in the first place.

The only time I've felt really attacked online was when two people started attacking my reputation after I'd been involved in organising a big event for a mental health charity. I was really tired when I started seeing the comments and messages coming through on the morning after the event. It was 9am and I'd been up all night.

I also thought it was incredible how people could be so nasty online towards someone who is doing something for mental health – the irony of it all. Maybe they didn't realise that 20 years ago I was married to a manic depressive who was very unwell, and it was an incredibly difficult time in my life. I had first-hand experience of living with severe mental health issues. We don't always know people's stories and a little kindness goes a long way in life. We have no control over what other people say or do, only our response and reaction. Initially, I was really upset by what I was reading, but then I caught myself.

Hang on, these people aren't my friends. I don't require their approval. I know what I've done and I know I've done it from a good place, and that the event was a success. Who cares what they think? It's been a magnificent experience and the people who matter are the other volunteers I've worked with for months to pull this off. Those are the people who matter. Those other people can think what they want, but I can choose my response.

Instead of going to sleep feeling sad and angry, I focused on positive thoughts. I went through all the good that had come out of the event and how much I enjoyed working with the other people who had been involved in putting it together. When I woke up, I was met by a host of amazing comments from the volunteers and attendees, all talking about how wonderful the event was and how much they enjoyed it. Sometimes you have to tune out the haters so that you can turn up the volume on the people whose opinions matter.

SURROUND YOURSELF WITH SMART PEOPLE

This is good advice for business in general, not just for dealing with bullies and haters. Make sure you have a group of peers

Chapter 10: Dealing with Bullies and Haters

and a network like I have through my mastermind group. I also have a number of estate agent friends in Ireland who are a great support. I've met most of these agents through being a member of the IPAV. These networks are so important and the people you meet through them will be an invaluable support when you're facing a difficult situation. You don't have to do this on your own. Building a network of people with whom you can share the load will make every difficult situation you encounter a bit easier to handle.

If someone does threaten you, assess the situation and try to see it from their point of view. Is it valid? Are they just being supremely aggressive? Who can you get advice from? Break it down into all the worst-case scenarios and make sure you're covered for each one. Sometimes very reasonable clients can be unreasonable and that's different – always consider that maybe something has happened in their lives or that they're just having a bad day.

DON'T SWEAT THE SMALL STUFF

It can be really easy to get stressed out by the smallest things. When I look back at what I was worried about two years ago now, it feels like a vague and distant memory. Know that if you're doing your best and doing the right thing, then nothing else really matters. Ignore the haters – tune them out or block them from your social channels.

If you do make a mistake, own it. Apologise, make it right and learn from it. None of us are perfect and we shouldn't expect anyone else to be either. Don't sweat the small stuff, because it's really not worth it. Remember that you don't need anyone else's approval, but your own.

What I mean by that is if you're taking actions, doing your best and living by your values, keep doing it and don't worry what others think of you. As long as you know your reason for doing what you're doing, just keep going. When I was going through a difficult personal time, one of the most valuable tools I had was a very simple mantra: "I don't require your approval, I require my own approval." It was a powerful reminder that I was doing this for me, not for anyone else. I also knew I was doing the right thing.

To bring this back to my business, I'm sure there are people out there who think, "Who does Regina Mangan think she is? Would you look at her, always posting those videos on social

Chapter 10: Dealing with Bullies and Haters

media, I'm sick of hearing from her!" I'd say to those people, you're entitled to your opinion, but I know what I'm doing and why – we want to be helpful experts and promote Waterford as a wonderful place to live. I know I'm doing this from a good place, so if you don't like me, that doesn't matter and it's not my business.

If you worry too much about being judged, you'll never put yourself out there. You have to detach this personal need for approval from what you need to do for your business. This is especially important when it comes to putting yourself out there on social media, and doing videos like we do. So few agents produce videos that when you do, it really makes you stand out in the world of selling property. It's important to be professional but true to who you are. To be authentic you also have to show some vulnerability, and when you do you'll build trust with people much more easily. Can I suggest you follow Tom Panos – he's the number one estate agency coach and influencer in Australia. You will learn a lot from this man.

Focus on what matters in the grand scheme of things, rather than the small stuff. You can't worry too much about what other people will think, and as long as you're coming from a good place and doing your best, you can't go too far wrong.

DON'T HIDE FROM PROBLEMS OR DIFFICULT SITUATIONS

If you screw up or if you are facing a difficult situation don't hide from it, tackle it head on. This is really important because that problem isn't going to go away if you just ignore it. But tackling a difficult situation doesn't mean rushing in unprepared either. Think about the outcome you want to achieve. If you're going to have a meeting, think carefully about where you'll hold it and perhaps ask a colleague to join you.

If the person you're meeting is aggrieved, it's important that you allow them to share their frustrations. Sometimes people just want to vent and be heard. That doesn't mean it's acceptable for them to scream and shout, or to become physically intimidating, but you do need to hear them out. Listen to them and really hear what they're saying.

Don't let people make dirt of you – have your boundaries and standards, and stick to them. It all comes back to mutual respect. You want to give respect and you want to receive respect.

Chapter 10: Dealing with Bullies and Haters

TAKE A BREATH

It can take time to learn how to do this, but assess every situation as calmly as possible. Take a measured approach to the difficult situations you face and you'll find that you panic a lot less. If you feel yourself slipping into anxiety and stress, take a breath. You don't always need to have the answer straight away, so pause. That pause might last ten minutes, it might last 24 hours, just take the time you need to ensure you're never replying from a place of aggression or panic.

This will help you stay focused, which is essential as a business leader. It's vital that you protect your mindset and your mental and physical health. Whenever you're getting stressed and taking onboard all the negativity that can come from others, you're losing energy and you're closing yourself off from opportunities. Remember, business isn't all about the money, you've got to enjoy yourself too. Happiness is so important and, after all, this life is not a dress rehearsal.

Steps for success

- Set clear boundaries – know what behaviour is unacceptable and draw a line in the sand from the start of any relationship.

- Stand up to bullies – they're usually all talk, so ask yourself what's the worst they can do and take away their power over you.

- Be true to yourself – be yourself and your tribe will find you and follow you.

- Build your network – have access to a network of people who can provide you with advice and support.

CHAPTER 11

LIVE IN THE NOW

I'm going to be completely honest with you and say upfront that I am pretty rubbish at living in the now – but it's something I'm working on and something that I have become a lot more mindful of in the last few years. Living in the now really means being present in whatever you're doing. It's particularly important when you're interacting with other people, but living in the now also has a positive impact on your own happiness and wellbeing.

I have to actively work on being present because my natural default is to pack as much as possible into every day. I used to be guilty of squeezing as many appointments and calls into my diary as I could. That might feel like an efficient way of working, but the downside was that I wasn't always truly present in any of my interactions with other people. What's more, I was driving my own anxiety and stress levels up by trying to fit too much in – all it took was one call to run over by ten minutes and then I'd be racing to catch up.

Picture the scene, I've been talking on my hands-free kit in the car after dropping my son at school. I'm a couple of minutes from the office and I decide I have time to make just one more call. I direct my phone to dial the next person I need to speak to and we're in full flow as I'm parking my car. I hop out, still having a conversation, and walk briskly into the office. I give my colleagues in the office a cursory wave and a smile as I come through the door, while still chatting on the phone and looking for the paperwork I need for my first appointment of the day. By the time I hang up, I'm already heading out of the door for my first appointment – it's a never-ending cycle of calls and appointments, and during each one my mind is racing ahead to the next thing I "need" to do.

One day I stopped myself from making that extra call. I thought about how I'd feel if I was working on reception and other people breezed in on their phones, barely even acknowledging

Chapter 11: Live in the Now

me each morning. I realised that this doesn't give the people around me a nice experience and that I needed to be more present. This is when I started making a conscious effort – and make no mistake, this does not come easily to me – to be present in my interactions not just at work, but at home too.

For me, that meant not squeezing in "one more call" just as I was pulling up at the office or to pick my son up from school. I became much more mindful about how long the calls I was on would take and started thinking about when I would be in a place where I could be present on the end of the phone. This might sound incredibly basic, but it is something I wasn't consciously aware of for a very long time.

Although I don't think that the years I spent not being fully present have severely impacted my relationships, I do think it means there have been many occasions when I haven't shown up at my best. As a business owner, it is very easy to get caught up in the busyness of it all – everything feels urgent. Clients need you. Your team needs you. There's a deadline. You know how it feels! But there is so much value in taking a moment to pause, step back and look at what really does need your attention at that moment, and then be fully present with that person or in that task.

This is particularly important for relationship building. I do my best to make sure I am fully present whenever I walk into a room now. I make time to have a social conversation with people, because it's those moments of small talk that are so important for building rapport and developing relationships. This doesn't have to take a lot of your time, but it does require conscious thought.

For example, I go to the same coffee shop every morning on my way into the office. Amanda, who works there, is always friendly and always has my coffee ready for me as soon as I get to the counter. In the past I'd rush in on my phone, grab my coffee, pay and leave. One day as I was about to go in for my coffee, I realised I was on my phone again, but also that Amanda deserved my attention. I finished my call as I walked in and apologised for being on my phone.

At that moment I decided I wasn't going to let it happen again because these are magical moments with people in my world. I want to enjoy those moments with the people I interact with, whether they're making me a coffee and we're having a chat or they're another parent at the school gates wanting a chat while we wait for our children.

Chapter 11: Live in the Now

SWITCH OFF TO SHOW UP

As I've become more self-aware, I've realised the importance of switching off from work so that I am able to show up at my best in every area of my life. In the past, I would be working 24/7, but now I make time for myself and give myself opportunities to be present every day. A small change has been listening to music in my car on the way from the gym to the office in the morning, instead of immediately making calls. It's a small shift in my habits, but one that means when I do arrive at work, I am ready to be present there and in the zone.

This can be easier said than done, especially in the modern world where everyone expects answers immediately. You've got people calling your phone, emails coming in constantly and many other demands on your attention. This means you have to work really hard to stay present and be focused on what requires your attention at that moment in time, rather than being distracted by everything else that is competing for your attention and energy.

I've talked a lot throughout this book about the importance of having a long-term plan for the future. That doesn't change by shifting your mindset to one where you consciously focus on being present each day. In fact, being present allows you to take the small actions along the way that contribute towards your long-term plan.

This means you have to set yourself up for success by thinking about the environment you need to be in to accomplish different tasks. If you're having calls, for instance, you'll want a quiet space away from other people and you want to keep other distractions – like email or message notifications – to a minimum.

You also have to make sure you have time when you can switch off from work to spend with your family. When I go on holiday now, I don't answer my phone to work calls and my team keep all my emails for me to answer when I return. Everyone on my team knows that they can contact me with something urgent, and they also understand what urgent really means.

There have been occasions when I've needed to be contactable during a holiday, because I was working on a couple of big deals while I was away and couldn't step away completely, but when I need to do this I have become much better about setting clear boundaries. I'll choose when I am available for calls or meetings and I will stick to those times. As I said in

Chapter 11: Live in the Now

Chapter 2, this will improve your relationships with your clients and will lead to a greater level of mutual respect. Needless to say, sometimes "life happens", such as in the case of my last holiday when a team member was out on leave, which meant I had to take calls. In this instance, that was OK because that's not the norm – sometimes even the best-laid plans don't go to plan.

When you make sure you are fully present for the people you are interacting with, you show that you respect their time and energy. In doing so, you also encourage them to respect you. As I've said, being present often only takes small shifts in our behaviour, but it can have a big impact on how other people feel about your interactions and, therefore, about you.

By setting boundaries, and abiding by the boundaries other people set, you are building a relationship built on respect. This sets you up for success from the beginning of your interactions, particularly in business relationships. If you constantly allow a client to contact you out of hours, not only is it not good for your stress levels or personal life, but it often leads to resentment of that person, and that is only going to damage your relationship in the long term.

TREAT PEOPLE WITH KINDNESS

Kindness should never be undervalued and it goes a long way. Small acts of kindness cost nothing, whether you're giving your seat on the train to someone who needs it more than you or you're helping someone cross the road. Think about how it makes you feel when you experience a nugget of kindness like that in your day – don't you want to make other people feel like that too?

Sometimes we can all be guilty of being selfish because we're so busy, but kindness and consideration is so important – and you never know when you may need someone else to show that kindness to you. I often think back to the day I collapsed in the pharmacy – I'll talk more about this in the next chapter. The extraordinary compassion and kindness these strangers showed me when I was lying on the floor feeling like I might die really touched me and it's made me even more determined to be kind whenever I can in my life.

As an example, while I was writing this book, I went to look at a house in West Waterford that had been on the market with another agent for about eight months. In that period, I'd sold two houses on the same estate, and it didn't take me long to

Chapter 11: Live in the Now

realise why the houses I'd marketed had sold while this one hadn't. The photos of the property in the advert were terrible – the house looked dark, there was clutter in the rooms and it wasn't presented at its best.

The lady who owned it contacted me after I sold these two other properties nearby. During our appointment she was very emotional and cried at times, because she needed to leave the house for personal reasons. I knew she needed our help, and when we take on any property it's never about the fee, it's about supporting each client on their journey and achieving a happy ending for them. When you do this, the fees follow. In this particular case, I told the lady that she needed to take the house off the market and "rest" it while she got it ready to sell.

I said that the house needed to be repainted, with all the rooms painted white rather than the dark colours they were currently, to help bounce the light around. I also told her that the carpet on the stairs needed replacing. "I can't afford to replace the carpet," she told me through her tears.

"Look, I will move mountains to sell this house for you, but if you want to leave this house you have to change the carpet," I replied. Whenever we take on a new property, we charge a marketing fee, but in this case I told her that I'd waive our marketing fee so that she could afford to replace her carpet. It might sound cheesy, but this isn't about our fees. It's a privilege to help this lady and her children move on by getting them out of that house.

It is important to point out that there's a big difference between being kind and being a sucker – there are occasionally clients who can more than afford our marketing fee but who don't want to pay it, which is very different. There will be people who try to take advantage of your kindness, but they are in the minority.

When you give, and it's coming from a good place, you can't go too far wrong. We work in residential housing and we can't accommodate everyone who comes our way, but that doesn't mean we can't be kind, even to those we can't directly help.

For instance, a lady came into our office recently looking for a rental property. She had a baby in a buggy with her and was quite flustered. She didn't have any references, so I knew we'd find it hard to get her a property, but I didn't just send her on her way. I made her a coffee, told her to take a seat and to relax. We chatted and I gave her the number of a local councillor who

Chapter 11: Live in the Now

is in my circle and who might be able to help her find somewhere to live. This introduction proved very helpful for this lady. When she left, she told me she felt a lot better. These small gestures are often what make the biggest difference to people's experiences.

GIVERS GAIN

You gain when you give and, for me, this approach ties back into our values. Empathy and doing the right thing are two of our values and both encourage us to act with kindness. Empathy is particularly important for building relationships with your team, your clients and the broader community.

When you think about how kindness can show up in your business, consider the kind of culture you want to create. If your team sees you extending empathy and kindness to others, you would hope they would follow your lead and do the same. When you lead from the front, your kindness ripples out and spreads further than it could on its own. This all has an impact on the environment you create for your team and, therefore, how they show up at work for one another and for your clients.

What kind of place would you like to work in? I know someone who works for a business that wouldn't let them take time off when their partner was seriously ill. That's awful – and I don't think anyone wants to work somewhere with that kind of toxic culture. Did you know that culture is the biggest area people want to change in the companies they work for? Research from Gallup found that 41 per cent of employees said changing the culture or engagement at their workplace would improve their lives more than a pay rise. Among job seekers, although increased pay was the most important thing they were looking for, improved wellbeing and opportunities to grow and develop were next on the list.[7]

When you set up your business, the kind of culture you're going to create is one of the things you need to decide, because your workplace culture starts with you. Come back to your values and mission. Remember why you got into business. Are you living your values? If not, why not? What can you do to make sure your values are at the heart of everything you do?

---

7   Gallup, Inc. (2023) *State of the Global Workplace Report - Gallup, Gallup.com.* https://www.gallup.com/workplace/349484/state-of-the-global-work-place.aspx#ite-506915.

Chapter 11: Live in the Now

More and more of us are in business not only to make money, but because we have a greater purpose. We want to do good in the world, have a positive impact and leave a lasting legacy. We want to give back to our community and champion Waterford as a wonderful place to live. It's part of our corporate social responsibility (CSR), but this has been a focus for us at Liberty Blue long before I ever heard that specific term.

For years we have run an annual coffee morning in aid of St Vincent de Paul, a charity that helps tackle poverty in local communities. We have always wanted ours to be a huge success and it's honestly a highlight of our year. Does it take up a lot of time, energy and effort to organise? Yes. Is it worth it? Absolutely! We love doing something meaningful that actually makes a difference to people's lives – not only do we raise money for a very worthy cause, but we also host a fun event where people can mingle, socialise and take time to connect with others in our community.

This is all part of how we show up and are present in our community. We love doing it, so it has a positive impact on us, but more importantly it has a positive impact on others, and this is what you will be remembered for. I know it's what I want to be remembered for, because while building a business is important and has been a huge part of my life, I want to leave a lasting and positive legacy. It's all part of my attitude of gratitude and looking for opportunities to give back wherever I can.

NOTHING IS GUARANTEED

As I've got older, I've become much more aware of my own mortality, as I think many of us do. Going to funerals in particular is very sobering, especially when they are for your peers, because it reminds you not to take anything in life for granted. Tomorrow isn't guaranteed for any of us.

My mentor Sanjay Gandhi was recently diagnosed with a rare form of cancer called Chordoma. He has hugely inspired the world of estate agents, and has chosen to speak about his illness and to share his journey in finding the best neurosurgeon in the UK. Not only that, but despite his illness he organised a conference for estate agents in September called Sanjfest. The guest speakers were Tom Panos, Lisa Novak and Josh Tesolin, and it was hosted by the formidable Christopher Watkins. The conference not only gave world-class insights into what the best agents do in a tough market, but also acted

Chapter 11: Live in the Now

as a fundraiser for Bone Cancer Research Trust. How incredible is Sanjay, this human who inspires me every day?

I know I'm a big planner, and I'm always looking to the future, but I'm very conscious that you never know what the future will bring, either for yourself or the other people you care about in life. It can be really easy to let opportunities to spend time with your friends and family pass you by – life is busy, it's understandable. But I know my relationships with my closest friends are really important to me and contribute greatly to my happiness, so I try to prioritise them.

This ties into what I've already discussed about living in the now – we all need to prioritise the relationships that are important to us, whether with friends or family, and maintaining those relationships plays a big role in creating the right balance in our lives. In the past I've been guilty of not staying in touch with people and not giving some of my friends the time and energy they deserve – or not being fully present when I am with them.

Nowadays, I'm reinvesting my time and energy into my friends and family. I take nothing for granted and I see spending quality time with them as not only an investment in our relationship,

291

but also as an investment in my happiness. To make sure I spend time with people, it goes in my diary.

How often have you bumped into a friend you haven't seen for ages in the street and said, "I'll call you to get a catch up in the diary…" only to fail to make that call or send a message to organise something. I strongly believe that if you want to meet up with someone, you should get your diaries out then and there to plan it. Book that time, commit to those relationships. I know how hard it can feel when you're busy, but I can't stress enough the importance of spending time with the people you love for your overall health and wellbeing.

All of this feeds back into our businesses too, because if we're going to show up as successful entrepreneurs we need to be in our happy zone and take time out to refresh our energy. If we are always working, we don't get the rest we need and we don't top up our energy levels. Sometimes we need to slow down and take time out to allow us to speed up.

If, as you've been reading this, you know that you're guilty of prioritising work above all else and you don't take enough time out for yourself and your friends and family, I invite you to take this opportunity to pause and just think about what makes you

Chapter 11: Live in the Now

happy. Who are the most important people in your life and how can you build time into your week to spend with them when you're fully present?

This doesn't have to mean setting aside hours of your day when you're not working. Think about the pockets of time you already have in your day with your children, your partner or your friends and really focus on being fully present during those periods. It might be on the journey to school in the morning with your children, mealtimes with your family or a quick coffee after a gym session with your best friend. In those little moments, put your phone away. Ignore the beeps and instead focus on the person in front of you – this is coming from someone who has to work hard at this.

Similarly you can set aside time during your day to focus on your work, which will allow you to show up fully for your business and your team. Creating those boundaries and pockets of time for different relationships and activities will help you find a better balance in your life and ultimately mean that you are happier and more fulfilled at home and at work.

Steps for success

- Be present – think about how you can show up at your best for everyone in your life and remove distractions when you're interacting with others.

- Slow down – are you cramming too much into your days? What can you take out of your diary to give you time to slow down and be present, and in doing so accelerate your success?

- Be kind – kindness costs nothing, but it leaves a huge positive impact. Treat others with compassion and kindness whenever you can.

- Live now – take nothing for granted and make sure you diarise time to spend with the people you care most about.

CHAPTER 12

MANAGING CHANGE

As anyone who's been in business for any amount of time will know, things constantly change. Certainly in our business it's always about change because we are working on continuously improving. There have been more changes in the business over the years than I can mention here – from personal change like pregnancy and managing the business around that, to expanding from rentals into sales. We've rebranded, we've moved offices and we've introduced new technology. The list goes on!

Sometimes we've experienced pushback from the changes we've made – introducing 14 new pieces of technology in four years was one example, but that didn't stop us moving forwards and it's not only worked, but it's revolutionised our business. Of course, when Covid-19 hit, which was two to three years after this big shift in the business, all of our team had aha moments and realised how far ahead of our competitors we were, as a result of pushing through the discomfort of that change.

What gave Maria and I the confidence to implement that change and overcome the objections and excuses some of the team had, was that we'd seen what good looked like when we visited Kristjan at Base. The time we spent in his office gave us such a clear vision and once we committed to making those changes in our business, we were unapologetic about it.

Of course, we didn't introduce all 14 new pieces of software in one go – we rolled them out gradually over the course of three to four years, giving everyone time to get used to the new ways of working before introducing the next new piece of technology. One of the other ways we helped the wider team buy into these changes was to take them to Kristjan's office so that they could also see the vision we were aiming for. Once they could also clearly see what good looked like, they were more motivated to support the changes we introduced.

Chapter 12: Managing Change

Changing for the better

When I started working on this book in January 2023, our business looked quite different. In the ten months I've been working on this project so far, there have been a host of changes within the business.

One of the most significant has been outsourcing our entire accounts department, which has made the business much more efficient and saved us a lot of money, not to mention removing a lot of stress. We have also outsourced renewing our estate agency licence, which seemed a big deal when we did it in-house, but with this new approach it feels much faster and more efficient.

Our general manager John started in the business a couple of months before I started writing this book and his input has been huge. He fits in really well with the team and has taken a lot of the day-to-day people management off my plate. He has introduced KPIs for every member of the team, which means everyone is clear on what's expected of them, he holds bi-weekly one-to-ones with everyone and they all have clear plans for their professional development and growth. John is great at managing and this has increased happiness levels across the whole business.

We have also hired two South Africa-based VAs, thanks to the advice from my amazing mentor Sanjay, and they are working incredibly well for the business. Since Vereisha took over the management of our maintenance, this division is the most efficient it's ever been and that's contributing to an increase in our financial growth as a business.

Not all changes have to be big — like new hires or outsourcing entire departments. One of the most effective changes we've made in 2023 is introducing daily team meetings. This has had an enormous impact on the business, helping everyone feel more connected and giving everyone a chance to share what's going on in their day, as well as get support with any challenges or problems they're facing. The two girls in South Africa also join via video, which helps make them feel connected to the rest of the team, all of which helps everyone feel happier.

Chapter 12: Managing Change

A POSITIVE PERSPECTIVE ON CHANGE

Change is inevitable and personally I love it, because to me change means improvement. I love getting better, making things more efficient and working on continuous improvement, both for myself and the business. I think my love of change comes from my entrepreneurial side – I'm not just an estate agent, I'm a business owner.

That said, I don't want to change things just for the sake of it. It's important to take a measured approach to change. I like coaching the people around me to bring them on that journey of change with me.

It's important to recognise the improvements in the business as a result of the changes we've made too. For instance, in the last 12 months we've increased our profit margins by 10 per cent through the changes I have already explained in this book. When you have results like that, you can show everyone in the business that these changes matter and have a positive impact.

EMBRACING CHANGE WITHOUT SACRIFICING YOUR WELLBEING

While I love change and making improvements to the business and personally, that's not to say that sometimes change can't be difficult. I find I'm most likely to become stressed or overwhelmed with change when it's not something I've planned for. As an example, recently a key person in the business has needed to take several months off for compassionate leave. There's no denying that's been a cause of stress, but because of some of the other changes we've already made this year – like bringing John onboard as our general manager – this has been much easier to manage than it would have been.

Change might be inevitable, but sacrificing your own wellbeing to adapt to it doesn't have to be. I have certainly learned from my own experiences in recent years that it's important to keep an eye on my own wellbeing to prevent me from burning out...

I freely admit that I took my health and fitness for granted before I entered my 50s. I assumed that if I exercised, ate well and lived a good life then I would be well, but I've learned that even if you do everything right (and I'm not saying I was

Chapter 12: Managing Change

doing everything right, but I wasn't doing badly!), nothing is guaranteed.

Things all started changing for me during the Covid-19 pandemic. During the first lockdown I was walking lots and still feeling pretty well, but I worked too hard – I was terrified of losing business during the lockdown (as I'm sure many business owners were), so I put in a lot of extra grind.

During the lockdowns, we focused on what we could do for the business, such as writing our operations manuals and preparing more marketing than we ever had before. We threw ourselves into the change, but it was hard at times. With the estate agency sector essentially closed, there were difficult decisions to make. I had to make two people redundant, while also trying to keep the rest of the team motivated. This, more than anything, took a toll on my mental health.

I also caught Covid not once, but three times during this period, which severely impacted my physical health. I fooled myself into thinking that if I was working on my laptop in bed, I was resting. At the time, I didn't realise just how much energy I was expending by being mentally switched on all day – I might have changed my routine, but I wasn't supporting my wellbeing.

301

After a few months, I realised I had long Covid. I felt unwell all of the time. Every time I started to feel better, I'd start doing things, but that would then tip me back into being unwell. It was an incredibly frustrating and debilitating cycle to be in for the best part of a year and a half. Mentally this had a huge impact on me, because I'm such a high-energy person and I love to have plans. I started to feel more and more depressed.

But long Covid wasn't my only health concern. I also had to undergo surgery to remove a benign lump from my neck because it had been steadily growing. It had reached about the size of a fist, so the consultant advised me that it was necessary to remove it otherwise it would cause problems. I had the operation in May 2022, and I didn't appreciate how much that would take out of me – and I'll admit I probably didn't rest as much as I should have when I was recuperating.

I had (optimistically as it turned out) booked myself onto a yoga retreat in Portugal in September 2022. I thought it would be really good for me to get away and focus on myself for a week, but life had other plans.

A few days before I was due to travel, I was in Waterford when I started to feel incredibly unwell and got what I'd describe as

Chapter 12: Managing Change

bad vertigo. Everything was moving around me, I could barely stand up and then I collapsed in the pharmacy. At that moment, I thought I was going to die. It was terrifying. I was put in an ambulance and spent five days in hospital – needless to say I didn't make it to my yoga retreat!

This was my body's way of telling me to stop. It took about seven to eight months for me to recover from the surgery to remove the lump, but by the beginning of 2023 I was starting to feel better. However, I wasn't going to take this for granted again, so I looked for support to help me get better and stay well. Just as you need a support network in business, you need one for your health and wellbeing too.

I now see an acupuncturist every week, I have a personal trainer at the gym and I hired an accountability coach to help me stay on track with my nutrition and diet. In the past, these kinds of appointments would have been nudged out of my diary because I'd have told myself I didn't have time to go to them. Now I've flipped my perspective – I tell myself I don't have time *not* to go.

Why have I told you all of this? Because as business owners we have a tendency to push through no matter what. We don't stop and we often don't prioritise our own wellbeing and health. We put our business before ourselves, but that's only ever going to lead to health problems and burnout. The wonderful thing is that when you put yourself first and take care of yourself, you're happier and that leads to a happier team and a higher-performing business.

However, you need to have the resources, systems and processes in place to allow you to have that space from your business. This is when everything I've talked about so far in this book comes into play – you need the right people on your bus, ones who align with your values and vision; you need to carry out thorough training for all of your staff; you need documented processes that your team can follow; you need systems in place within your business. When you have all of this, you are well on your way to having a business that can not only run, but perform at a very high level, without you.

Ultimately, by doing everything I've already talked about you are setting yourself up for success and this allows you the space you need to disconnect. For example, since we hired John as our general manager in November 2022, I've been able to take a week off and completely unplug. I know,

Chapter 12: Managing Change

operationally, he has everything in hand and that has enabled me to disconnect.

The benefits of having this time off have been huge – I came back from my holiday feeling fresher, happier, more focused and well rested. All of that means I perform better for my business and my team, as well as feeling better in myself.

KNOW YOUR LIMITS

Listen to your body – having ignored mine for too long I can't stress enough how important this is. The body gives us signals to tell us when it's tired or when something is wrong. Instead of pushing through, and thinking it will "sort itself out", pause, think about what's really going on and act on the information your body is giving you.

It might be knee pain when you're doing a certain exercise at the gym, or it might be that you're falling asleep at your desk in the middle of the afternoon. I wasn't always good at this, but I'm getting much better and I find that seeing people like my acupuncturist (who is also a physiotherapist) really helps. I go to her every single week, which is me investing in me.

My trainer Ross at the gym really helps too – he will modify my training regime to suit my body as it is now, rather than what I think my body should be able to do based on how it was five years ago.

One small example is that I've always loved pushing the prowler in the gym – ram on the weights and off she goes! But my body is telling me I can't do that any more. A year ago, that would probably have really upset me, but now that I've adopted an attitude of gratitude, I'm grateful for what my body *can* do. I don't want to get injured and not be able to train at all, so I've accepted that I have to stop pushing the prowler and instead modify my exercise routine. I'm listening to my body – it's really no different to listening to your business, being agile and manoeuvring around whatever the world throws your way.

For example, we changed the way in which we book property viewings to help protect mine and the other agents' energy. So, we will now build up viewings for a property we're selling so that they are all happening on the same day, back to back. This might sound counterintuitive if you're thinking about protecting your energy, but in fact this works really well because instead of spending time driving back and forth to the same property multiple times a week, you're able to make that

Chapter 12: Managing Change

journey only once. We're confident in our service and in our knowledge, and we have set up the pre-marketing and technology that ensures this works well. We're working smarter, faster and better. Of course, you have to adjust along the way to suit your business and client needs.

EMBRACE CHANGE AND LOOK TO THE FUTURE

If, as a business owner, you are fearful of change, you are likely to be left behind. There are certainly some dinosaurs in the world of estate agencies, but if you're reading this book I'm willing to bet you're not one of them! The key is to embrace change and always think about change in the context of how you want to grow your business – when you have a plan for where you want to go and what you want to achieve, it's much easier to see what changes are required to get you there.

Although none of us can predict what's going to happen, we still need to look at how we can future-proof our businesses and keep one eye on what's coming around the corner. As I write this, the cost of living is increasing in Ireland, interest rates are going up and we can see that the UK estate agency market is dipping, which is our nearest market. As a business, we're looking at how we can increase our recurring revenue, as well as making a plan for the training we need for our team to help future-proof our operations. As an example, we've put two of our team into estate agency college studying auction-eering, which is a two-year programme, so that we have more licenced agents in the business in the future. This also shows that we are keen to develop and motivate the talent within the business, which can help us attract more high-quality staff in the months and years ahead. We want everyone to know that this is an exciting place to work.

We're also using our marketing, and in particular our videos, to make sure we stand out from other agents and are sharing what's truly unique about us. We need to leverage and capital-ise on our differences to help us stay one step ahead.

I've also spoken to two estate agents recently who are both leaving the firms they work for to set up on their own, and nei-ther of them are going to rent an office space. I've told them that I think this is wise, because an office is a huge expense and nowadays it's not an essential one.

Chapter 12: Managing Change

As an established estate agent that presents a risk, because the way in which we do business online nowadays, as well as the rise of social media, means there will be more competition in the estate agency industry and that competition will increasingly come from members of this younger generation who have started their businesses harnessing technology and, therefore, typically have much lower overheads than those of us that have been around longer.

Even though we have no intention of getting rid of our office completely, we are intending to move away from a high-street location to one in a business park where we can get lower rates, and where there is plenty of parking for our staff and customers. The point is, our business has evolved and improved to the point that we don't need footfall in order to attract either tenants for rental properties or buyers and sellers. So much of our process is automated, can be carried out online by scanning a QR code on one of our signs, or both, that there's no need for many potential clients or tenants to visit our office at all.

This is all about looking for ways to improve, and ultimately looking for ways to reduce costs and do things more efficiently. Remember Tony's mantra of reduce, eliminate, automate? What costs can you reduce? What activities can you automate or even eliminate? What will that do for the profit in your business if you do?

SUPPORT SYSTEMS
FOR FUTURE IMPROVEMENT

The idea of needing to continuously improve and evolve as a business isn't new, but that doesn't mean it can't feel overwhelming at times. This is why having a mentor or coach who you trust is invaluable, as you can use them as a sounding board to help you work out what changes will lead to improvements for your business, and which ones will be a distraction. As I said earlier, this isn't about changing for the sake of it, it's about changing to improve the efficiency and profitability of the business.

In a similar way, it's important that you think carefully about who you're spending time with outside of work – who is in your circle of trust? These are the people you spend the most time with and, ideally, they will all be positive people who inspire you. When you have a circle of trust made up of inspiring, positive people, your mental health will be better and you'll

Chapter 12: Managing Change

have people who can help you distinguish the impactful improvements from the ineffective ones.

When I look at my circle of trust, it contains many people who inspire and help me: my husband, my mentor and friend Sanjay, my colleagues Maria and John, my personal trainer Ross, my acupuncturist Caroline, my cousin Denise, my friends Sheila, Grace and Aisling and a few more. I also have a couple of really great friends who have faced adversity of their own and continued driving on – these people are all incredibly positive and they encourage me to be better every single day just by being part of my life.

The lesson here is to be mindful of who you're spending the majority of your time with and if you notice that the people in your circle spend a lot of time complaining and, therefore, tend to drain your energy, consider how you can build a new circle that will set you up for success. You want to have industry role models who you admire – mine are people like Lisa Novak, Sanjay, Sean Barrett, Matt Giggs and a few more – as well as mentors who are based locally and know the market in which you're operating.

Your mentors are the people who can help you on your journey of improvement – they can help you work out what it is that you need to change, and then help you create a plan for getting there. Remember that change won't happen overnight, it takes time and you need to start small and roll new things out gradually. As the saying goes, how do you eat an elephant? Bite by bite. Talk to your mentors and others in your circle of trust to help you prioritise the changes you want to make – this will form the basis of your plan.

You can't rush this process, especially if you want to bring everyone on your team with you. We took four years to implement all the new pieces of technology we wanted to bring into the business, and we started with one that we knew would have a significant positive impact. For us, that was InventoryBase for carrying out property inspections – it didn't take long before everyone on the team was talking about how amazing the app was and how much easier it made their lives. They were reaping the rewards of this change and that made them much more open to future changes we introduced.

Always keep in mind the improvements you want to see in your business as a result of any change you make. Know your why. Know what good looks like. As I've said before, success leaves a

Chapter 12: Managing Change

trail, so find a mentor or role model whose trail you can follow to help you improve your business.

THE FUTURE FOR LIBERTY BLUE

I've shared many examples of how we've changed the business over the years, but I'd also like to share what we're focusing on in the 12 months after I've written this book. One area of focus is the sustainability of the business – I want us to be as environmentally friendly as we can in everything we do. It's a culture we're keen to build within the business.

We want to become an attraction agent, for both customers and talent. What do you want to focus on in the future? When it comes to customers, what type of customers do you want to attract? In terms of talent, what type of people do you want to attract and how will you do this? Although the business' profits are important for all of us, ask yourself, is it all about the money? Do you want to attract high-calibre people onto your team and how will you create a great working environment to retain talent?

CONTINUOUS IMPROVEMENT PAYS OFF

If you have any doubts about making changes and improvements in your business, let me tell you that, on reflection, for every single improvement we've made in the business there has been a time when I've gone to Maria and said, "Thanks be to God we did that." That's true whether I look back at the software we introduced years before the Covid-19 pandemic that enabled us to work remotely with minimal disruption, or hiring John as our general manager and investing in his training in the months before a key member of the team needed to take a few months off.

Every investment we've made, whether in hiring and training new people, new technology, or our online marketing activity has paid off. I can see it working and I trust the process. Everything we've done to improve and change has been hugely instrumental to the business thriving and has been important for my own sanity, particularly around the pandemic when the technology we'd introduced meant we could continue to trade when many estate agencies were unable to.

My advice to you is to trust the process, and make the effort to invest in business improvements, bite by bite, because you

Chapter 12: Managing Change

will see the benefits. No business should stay the same – regardless of the industry we're in, we have to find ways to evolve and we have to be willing to adapt. It's the only way to not only survive, but thrive.

Steps for success

- Embrace change – it will come whether you want it or not, so keep looking for ways in which you can improve and stay ahead of the curve.

- Schedule time for you – make your wellbeing and your health a priority; if you burnout you won't be able to serve your business.

- Surround yourself with people who inspire you – these people will support you, help you manage and introduce improvements and can show you what good looks like.

- Keep learning – educate yourself about new technologies and ways of working. By seeing what's coming around the corner, you can better prepare for the future and find new ways to improve efficiency in your business.

CONCLUSION

There you have it. Those are what I consider to be the most important lessons I've learned in the 26-plus years I've been in business. Although I've broken them down into 12 chapters, there are certain themes that come up repeatedly and these, more than anything else, are what I'd like you to take away from this book.

It all starts with **knowing your mission and values**. What's your purpose? Why are you in business? What impact do you want to have? What legacy do you want to leave? Once you are clear about your mission, define your values. These will act as a compass for you and your team. They'll help you make

Conclusion

better decisions and they'll help you stay true to who you are and what you stand for.

Once you know your mission and values, you can apply the **"begin with the end in mind"** principle from *The 7 Habits of Highly Effective People*. It is so much easier to work out what you need to do right now when you know what outcome you want to achieve. This is true whether you're working out how to have a difficult conversation with a client or colleague, deciding whether to develop and launch a new service, or indeed whether to sell your business for the best possible price.

You can also apply this principle to the next one – "**developing a culture of continuous learning**". Make time to learn about what is new and evolving in the world of residential property, beyond the changes to regulations and legislation that you need to know to stay in business. Encourage your team to build learning into their weeks as well. When you all do this, you'll be amazed at the innovation you unleash and the efficiencies you introduce. You'll also be building a strong culture and that can be very powerful.

Of course, learning is only beneficial if you **take action**. Knowing something will only get you so far if you don't implement what

Conclusion

you've learned and share it with others. Set metrics and schedules for actions. Check in on how people are progressing with their tasks and encourage everyone in your team to hold one another (including you) accountable for taking action in different areas.

In business, as in life, you can't escape change. Rather than fearing it, **see change as an opportunity for improvement** and embrace it. When you take the time to identify the right improvements for your business, and invest in getting buy-in from your team, you'll reap the rewards in more ways than one.

Finally, don't underestimate **the power of mentors**. I am not exaggerating when I say that I wouldn't have achieved half the level of success we have had I not had various mentors throughout my career. I've mentioned many of them throughout this book. Mentors are the not-so-secret ingredient to accelerating your success. By learning from others you gain invaluable insights about what works and what doesn't. You have access to a whole world of new perspectives and, perhaps most crucially, you can avoid the mistakes your mentors have made on their journeys.

Conclusion

"Mentoring is a brain to pick, an ear to listen and a push in the right direction," as John C. Crosby says.

That's not to say you won't make mistakes of your own. I'm sure you will and I know I certainly have. However, my mentors have helped me sidestep some huge landmines over the years. They've opened my eyes to new ways of working. They have challenged me, and still do. They've inspired me to keep striving to become *smarter, faster and better.*

Mentors will help focus your learning and will share their knowledge about areas of business that you may know nothing about. They will question you and your ideas to help you see new perspectives. They will inspire you to reach new levels of success.

What I'd like to know now that you've finished reading this book, is what action are you going to take? Or what action have you already taken as you've been reading? We can have all the coaching and mentoring in the world, but unless we implement what we learn it's a waste of time. As my wise mentor Sanjay would say; "Its shelf development not self development!" when we don't take action.

Conclusion

I'd like to invite you to write down the action (or actions) you're going to take based on what you've read. If you'd like some added accountability, you can even share them with me – **reginaomangan@icloud.com** – I'd love to hear from you and learn what you're doing to level up your business and your team.

ABOUT THE AUTHOR

Like a bracing south-westerly breeze, Regina Mangan blew into Waterford from County Limerick in 1995 with a handful of years' experience in hospitality management and a headful of ambition.

She had been hired to run Waterford's first apartment hotel, the Adelphi Wharf Suites – a challenge that she took on with gusto and completed successfully. This experience of innovation in business sparked Regina to develop her own first – the first property and letting management company: *Bookaroom.ie*

About the Author

It occurred to Regina that the skills used in hospitality are those that should be used in property – excellent customer service, efficiency and communication. Her research into the market showed that these skills would help her succeed in the property sector, giving her a clear way to stand out in the market and to compete.

From 1997 to 2014 *Bookaroom.ie* grew with Regina driving it on deftly through the many challenges that met it. Her energy, her focus on continuous upskilling and innovation, and the dedication to providing legendary customer service fuelled the development of the company so much so that in 2015 Regina and her team decided to expand into the property sales market.

Liberty Blue Estate Agents was the brand developed and made fabulous by Regina and her team to encompass both rentals and sales.

In the years preceding the Covid-19 crisis, Regina began a journey into the world of technology, innovation and social media marketing, culminating in Liberty Blue winning the regional category at the KPMG National Property Excellence Awards in 2019.

About the Author

Bringing her whole team with her through daily and weekly learning sessions, she not only made it possible for her company to survive the two years of lockdowns, but they also grew property sales income by 111% post Covid (*compared to 2019).

Regina lives in An Rinn, a Gaeltacht area in West County Waterford, with her son Pierce and husband Irial, who runs Nemeton TV. She is passionate about promoting Waterford City and County and in supporting the community she lives in.

Rotary, Pieta House and St Vincent de Paul are just a few of the organisations that Regina is passionate about supporting. Regina is a director of Waterford Chamber of Commerce, where she has been a business mentor for the Waterford Chamber of Commerce Leadership Program.

Regina loves working out in the gym and walking along the shore in beautiful An Rinn.

Printed by Amazon Italia Logistica S.r.l.
Torrazza Piemonte (TO), Italy

56354933R00190